MW01690468

DISCOVERING THE NEW COVENANT

WHY I AM NO LONGER A SEVENTH-DAY ADVENTIST

Greg Taylor

LIFE ASSURANCE MINISTRIES PUBLICATIONS
Glendale, Arizona

One Flock Ministries
10730 Bratton Court
Williamsport, Maryland 21795

Published by Life Assurance Ministries Publications
P.O. Box 11587
Glendale, Arizona 85318
(623) 572-9549 Information
(800) 355-7073 Orders only
Email: dale@ratzlaf.com
Web: www.ratzlaf.com

ISBN 0-9747679-0-5

CONTENTS

INTRODUCTION

The purpose of this book is three-fold. First, I wish to answer some questions often posed to me as a former minister in the Seventh-day Adventist Church. There are many Adventists who ask us, my wife and me, about our process out of the denomination. For many in that system the thought of leaving the church to join the larger Christian community is tantamount to apostasy from Christ. When we requested a transfer of our membership to the parish where we currently serve, our names were actually dropped from the Adventist Church records under the heading of apostasy. None of our former church members believed that we did not consider ourselves Christian. Nor did they consider any area of our lives to be immoral or out of harmony with the scriptural guidelines. Our "apostasy" status was based on the fact that the Adventist Church does not recognize other churches as a legitimate option for anyone who once held to the Adventist theological world view. Because of the teachings of the Adventist Church, many believe that salvation is at stake when one leaves. Most cannot understand that there could be any legitimate theological concern with what they believe is the truth. For these friends, family members, former members of churches we have pastored, and other concerned Adventists, we believe an explanation of our spiritual journey is important and is our personal responsibility.

Second, we are often asked questions by our Christian friends about the Seventh-day Adventist Church. Many of them have encountered Adventists and have questions about what they believe. Impressions of Adventists vary from respect for their hospital system, healthy lifestyle, and general clean living, to frustration or even anger over some of the criticism used in Adventist "evangelistic" methods that tend to discredit the legitimacy of the non-Adventist Christian community. In the middle, there is a high degree of curiosity and confusion in the Christian community about Adventism. Recent billboards that some well-meaning Adventists have placed around major cities in this country, equating Sunday with the mark of the beast, have triggered many questions, as well as a wide range of emotions. For these curious individuals I will attempt to share our personal journey through the Seventh-day Adventist system. Then I will share some of the reasons for our departure from it into the mainstream Christian community. Just what do Adventists believe and teach? This question and many others will be addressed in this book.

Finally, I have a deep heart for the unity in Christ of all of God's sincere, Bible believing people. Those of us who are deeply serious about our love for Jesus and for the great commission must learn to distinguish between that which is essential and that which is not. For the Christian church to be the evangelistic powerhouse Jesus intended in John 13-17, we must learn to pull together in love and unity for each other. This is not some ecumenical joining for political clout; far from it. I am referring to the unity of believers in passion for Jesus, love for one another, and radical obedience to the call to reach the world. There is nothing wrong with being part of a denomination, as long as that denomination realizes it is part of a greater body called the Church. We may have different functions in Christ's body, but we are all part of it. Denominationalism, on the other hand, is focused on perpetuating itself at the expense of other parts of the Christian church body. Such sectarianism is wrong and grieves the Lord deeply. I pray that this book will in a small way be an invitation to all who take the name of Jesus to stand strong for the unity of the Bride of Christ. Let us never allow any schism to divide us and dilute our effectiveness in our calling to reach the world.

Greg Taylor

DEDICATION

To my wife, Paula, who was willing to pursue the truth above comfort and security. Her dedication to following Jesus has been a tremendous source of strength for me, and I am most grateful. I also wish to thank my sons, Jordan and Matthew, for their courage to face questions, misunderstanding, and their own personal trauma as their family left the security of a well-established career and position in the community. Most of all, I want to thank my Lord Jesus for granting me a deeper understanding of His amazing grace and the joy of true rest in Him. For this I will be eternally grateful!

ACKNOWLEDGMENTS

I wish to extend special thanks to Lenora Marx for her special help in preparing this book for print. She spent many hours going over the manuscript, making suggestions, additions, and deletions. I could not have done it without her. I would also like to thank the many others who took time to share their thoughts and suggestions.

CHAPTER ONE

The Adventist Dilemma

The Seventh-day Adventist Church has brought confusion to Christians as long as it has been in existence. On the one hand, it appears to be a fully Christian denomination with some unique scriptural interpretations. On the other hand it does have some similarities to certain cultic groups, such as the Mormons and the Jehovah's Witnesses. This has caused many evangelicals to classify Seventh-day Adventists [SDA(s) or Adventist(s)] as a cult. Others have a much more inclusive sense about Adventists and believe they should be considered a unique but fully vested part of the body of believers called the Christian church. I will attempt to shed some light on this discussion as one who was born and raised in the Adventist Church, went through its private school system from first grade through post graduate study, and served as a pastor in that denomination for over 20 years (18+ years full-time). I continue to maintain significant friendships within that system and have a great appreciation for much that they represent. I believe I can share a balanced and objective perspective on the Seventh-day Adventist question that will be helpful for many who have questions or concerns related to it.

First, I want to make clear that in one primary respect, the Adventist Church is truly a Christian church. It believes in the full divinity of Christ. In spite of the fact that during the first decades of the church's existence a number of prominent Adventists taught that Jesus was the created Son of God, not the eternal God, by the end of the nineteenth century the church had clarified its position. Since then it has taught that Jesus was the pre-existent eternal Son of God and fully equal with God. In this Adventists differ from the Latter-day Saints and the Jehovah's Witnesses. They have a mainline Christian view of the Trinity. Adventists believe in the authority of the Scriptures as God's Word, justification by faith in Christ alone, the literal return of Jesus at the second coming (the reason for the Adventist part of its name), the resurrection of the just, the punishment of the wicked, and the importance of Godly living. Because of these truths held in common with other believers, many have accepted the Adventists into what is considered mainstream Christianity.

On the other hand, Adventists hold some unique doctrinal teachings that have puzzled the rest of the Christian community and have raised some theological eyebrows. Some of these are obvious, such as the celebration of the seventh-day Sabbath on Saturday. They believe that this observance is mandatory for all true Christians. They believe that the seventh-day Sabbath, as outlined in the fourth commandment, is binding for all time. And further, once this "truth" is understood, to ignore it is to be in rebellion against God. This is by far the most significant doctrine of the SDA Church. While Adventists teach that a person is justified by faith in Christ alone, they also believe that if one comes to the understanding of the seventh-day Sabbath and chooses not to observe it as a part of the sanctification process, that person will lose salvation and will at the end time receive the mark of the beast.[1] We will spend some significant time discussing how they understand this from their interpretation of the Scriptures in a later chapter.

Another doctrine that is highly visible is their emphasis on healthful living, specifically their adherence to the Old Testament dietary restrictions found in Leviticus chapter 11. They believe that these laws were part of the Old Testament system that had universal application. They consider any product that comes from swine (i.e. ham, bacon, pork), or any sea food that does not have fins or scales (i.e. shrimp, lobster, catfish, crab) is not only damaging to the body, but sinful. Many Adventists go further and promote a vegetarian lifestyle. While this is not a mandatory doctrine of the church, it is highly recommended in many segments of the church, and those who choose not to be vegetarian are considered second-class members.[2] Ministers are generally expected to be vegetarian as an example to the flock.[3]

Adventists also teach that in 1844 an investigative judgment began in heaven. They base this on a unique interpretation of Daniel 8:14, "Unto 2,300 days, then shall the sanctuary be cleansed." They connect various Scriptures to conclude that the judgment in heaven began on October 22, 1844. This is a complicated doctrine that we will examine later. It does, however, have great significance to the SDA Church It was the text that early Adventist William Miller originally interpreted to mean that Jesus would return to earth on this date. When Jesus did not appear, the segment of disappointed Adventists who now comprise the SDA Church, concluded that the cleansing of the sanctuary referred to a heavenly event that they called the investigative judgment. This doctrine is not shared with any other church or group. It is uniquely SDA. While there have been many

[1] Ellen G. White, *The Great Controversy*, p. 605 See also *Testimonies for the Church* Vol. 8, p. 117.
[2] Ellen G. White, *Counsels on Diets and Foods*, p. 36.
[3] Ibid. p. 399

dissenters over the years, and many key SDA theologians privately admit their doubts about its biblical validity, the church still proclaims this doctrine as one of its doctrinal pillars and part of its 27 fundamental beliefs. It is considered to be a test of fellowship. Most of their distinctive doctrines developed out of this core teaching.

The doctrine of "soul sleep," while also taught by some other Christians, is also considered a test of fellowship by Adventists. This doctrine teaches that when a person dies, the soul sleeps in the grave until Jesus comes. It does not go to heaven or hell directly at death, but sleeps until the resurrection. Adventists do not believe that the soul is immortal. They also do *not* believe that Hell will be an eternal place of punishment. They believe in a hell fire that has a beginning at the conclusion of the millennium and will last a matter of hours or days, rather than for eternity. This conditional immortality concept is not unique to SDAs. There are other Christians who are "conditionalist," but I know of none that make it a test of fellowship in their church or a dividing issue with other Christians.

Adventists are also noted for their early leader and co-founder, Ellen G. White (EGW). They believe that she was a prophet of God. Her prophetic gift is considered by Adventists to be one of the marks of their legitimacy from a biblical perspective. They teach that the "remnant church" spoken of in Revelation 12:17 refers to God's true last day church. They conclude from this verse that the last day church will be a commandment-keeping people (including the fourth commandment to keep Saturday, the seventh-day, as the Sabbath). It will have the "testimony of Jesus," which they link with Revelation 19:10, which reads, "For the testimony of Jesus is the spirit of prophecy." Therefore, they believe that because they keep the seventh-day Sabbath, Saturday, and they have a prophet, they are God's one and only "true church," or the "remnant church" of the last days. Ellen White's writings, (over 100,000 pages) are affectionately called by insiders "The Spirit of Prophecy." Did Ellen White consider herself to be a prophet? Yes, she did. While she did not put the label on herself directly, she did agree with those who called her a prophet. She stated that her work had an even greater weight of importance and responsibility than that of just a prophet.[4]

Ellen G. White's prophetic role in the Adventist Church has been confusing to other Christians. While Christians agree that there is a legitimate spiritual gift of prophecy, where does one draw the line between the biblical prophet and the spiritual gift? Adventists consider her a "continuing and authoritative source." This is one of the 27 fundamental beliefs that are required for membership. While they teach that the ultimate authority source is the Bible, they also believe that her writings are authoritative.[5] How does this play out in actual practice? Most Adventists will tell you that they believe in the Bible and the Bible alone for their practice, but they believe that Ellen G. White also has authority. So if a passage of Scripture is studied and there is any question about how it is to be interpreted, Ellen G. White's view will be considered the correct interpretation. Seventh-day Adventists will not claim openly that they have writings that are equal with Scripture, or a companion volume to it, as do the Mormons. However, in actual practice, they treat her writings in much the same way. The Adventists have produced their own version of the Scriptures, entitled *The Clear Word Bible* (CWB). (Later the word "Bible" was dropped from the title, so today it is called

---

[4] Ellen G. White, *Selected Messages*, Vol. 1 p. 36.

[5] *Seventh-day Adventist Church Manual*, 1990, p. 28 "One of the gifts of the Holy Spirit is prophecy. This gift is an identifying mark of the remnant church, and was manifested in the ministry of Ellen G. White. As the Lord's messenger, her writings are a continuing and authoritative source of truth which provide comfort, guidance, instruction, and correction. They also make clear that the Bible is the standard by which all teaching and experience must be tested."

The Clear Word.) This is a paraphrase by Jack Blanco in which Adventists have interpreted certain key texts to better reflect the opinions of Ellen G. White. This paraphrase was copyrighted and printed by the denominationally owned Review and Herald Publishing Association in 1994. While the forward in that Bible points out that it is a paraphrase, many people use it as an authoritative translation. Inside the dust cover is written, "Every text is phrased to make the original meaning as plain as possible to the modern reader." All one has to do is compare Daniel 8:12-14 in the CWB with another translation to see the obvious twisting of the original to fit the Ellen White world view. Many other examples could be given.[6]

One final point needs to be addressed. Seventh-day Adventists believe that they are *the one true church* of Bible prophecy, because commandment-keeping, including the seventh-day (Saturday) Sabbath, is one of the marks of that church. Because the Sabbath was the "seal" or "sign" of the 10 Commandment Law, it must be the Seal of God. Therefore, Adventists conclude that the mark of the beast must be Sunday worship. They believe that one day soon, when all of this comes to the forefront, all Christians will keep Saturday or they will receive the mark of the beast and be lost.[7] Anyone who leaves Adventism or has been introduced to the Sabbath but does not heed its warning, will be lost as well. It is this final claim that I will focus on primarily, as it is the key and most notable claim of the Seventh-day Adventist Church.

So what is one to conclude about the Seventh-day Adventist Church? Is it a mainline Christian church with a few unique doctrines or is it a cult, as some would contest? Before jumping to any conclusions, it is important to note

---

[6] For further comparisons see paper discussing *The Clear Word Bible* by Verle Streifling posted at www.Ratzlaf.com.
[7] Ellen G. White, *Spirit of Prophecy*, Vol. 4, p. 440-444

that there are many SDAs who are fine grace-oriented Christians. I would estimate that 25% of North American SDAs are truly evangelical. Many do not buy into the "remnant church" theory or believe that other Christians are less enlightened. There are many who do not hold Ellen G. White as an authority in Bible interpretation. Many keep Sabbath as a healthy lifestyle and not because they believe it is mandatory for all believers. But these people generally express their views cautiously behind closed doors. This is especially true among ministers and church employees where divergent views can adversely affect one's livelihood. The history of the Adventist Church is littered with stories of those who have been too outspoken on these issues. Even though their views were well supported by Scripture, they paid the price with loss of career and ostracism. It is this lack of safety for free expression within the church, and its exclusive views regarding other Christians, that are grounds for concern and require thorough investigation.

CHAPTER TWO

ADVENTIST UPBRINGING

I was born and raised in a conservative Adventist family. From my earliest years I can remember my parents reading *The Bible Story* books to me (Adventist publications often found in doctors' and dentists' offices) and teaching me the importance of obedience to God's laws, including the seventh-day Sabbath. *Uncle Arthur's Bedtime Stories* were also part of my upbringing. These books were filled with many great stories from the Bible and from life experience, yet they were heavily focused on behavior rather than on relationship. I grew up trying very hard to be good. I hoped to be pleasing enough to God to go to heaven. While many Adventists understand God's grace now, the era of my childhood and youth was highly performance oriented. We also read books by Ellen G. White. Some of my favorites as a child were books called *Early Writings* and *The Great Controversy.* In those books the dreams and visions of the Adventist prophet were written out. Also included were descriptions of the last days. I was fascinated by the stories and the descriptions of heaven. I was also impressed by the coming events of the end of time that Ellen White saw in vision. I enjoyed hearing about the history of the Adventist people and how things would be for them in the future. One part that scared me to death was the description of the judgment. We were told that we would have to be perfect when that time came because we would have to stand before God without a mediator.[1] We would have to be good enough to stand before God on our own merits.

I was taught that there would be great deception in the last days. There would be many false revivals. People would be caught up in these movements and would be led away from the truth. The only way we could be sure not to be deceived was be to pay attention to all that was written in the "Spirit of Prophecy" (Ellen G. White's writings), because those who lost faith in her inspiration would eventually reject the Sabbath and turn away from God and be lost.[2] I learned to be suspicious of any person or group who seemed to be having a deep experience with the Lord, because they might be getting caught up in a false revival. After all, Satan would imitate the miracles of God, and many could be led astray. We believed that the other churches were deceived by the Devil. They did not have the truth because they were disobedient to the fourth commandment. They should therefore be considered Babylon. Our duty as Adventists was to call the sincere believers out of Babylon into God's true remnant church. We would hold "evangelistic" meetings each year or sometimes more often than that. We felt it was our mission to get the people out of these nominal churches into the true church.

I also remember hearing the description of the persecution of those days. All the people of the world would turn against us and try to force us to keep Sunday.[3] Satan would appear and impersonate Jesus. He would deceive the nations into believing that Sunday was the true Sabbath. Those of us who refused to obey would be

---

[1] Ellen G. White, *Spiritual Gifts*, Vol. 1, p. 198
[2] Ellen G. White, *Testimonies for the Church*, Vol. 4, p. 211
[3] Ibid. Vol. 1, p. 201.

sentenced to death. There would be a national Sunday law in this country. Everyone who denied the true Sabbath and worshipped on Sunday would receive the mark of the beast. We would not be able to buy or sell if we did not keep Sunday. Finally, an execution day would be scheduled. Those of us who had not already been killed would be rounded up to be executed. Then Jesus would come at just the last moment and save the true Sabbath keepers. The rest would run to hide from the coming of the Lord. Only the true Sabbath keepers would be saved.[4]

Now, for those who have not been exposed to SDA eschatology this might seem rather bizarre. But this basic end-time teaching has not changed. Adventists are very careful not to disclose this initially, because they don't want to scare away potential converts. However, even today if one attends a *Revelation Seminar* or a *Prophecy Crusade* sponsored by the SDA Church the same scenarios are taught. For this reason the name "Adventist" is often hidden in the promotional materials, and meetings are often held in hotels or conference centers so as to hide the true identity of the sponsoring organization. At other times the event will be billed as one which is open to people of all denominations. This is done to disarm those that might be wary of the SDA name.

This end-time worldview was what I was taught as a child. I believed it with all my heart. I was both fascinated and terrified of the last days. As I grew older, I became more and more aware of my own inability to live a perfect life. I would confess my sins carefully each night and try to remember any that I might have forgotten. I remembered what Ellen White had said about people in the judgment

---

[4] Ellen G. White, *The Great Controversy*, p. 605
For a full description of the SDA worldview read the last five chapters of *The Great Controversy,* or the chapter entitled "The Loud Cry" in the *Spirit of Prophecy*, Vol. 4.

with an unconfessed sin on their record.[5] That single sin could mean being eternally lost. As I look at it now, I believe the primary reason I was so interested in these last day events was so that I could figure out how the events would transpire in order to know when I needed to get really serious about getting my life together. I might be able to gather enough strength to do a last minute sprint to the end. But I knew I could not be good enough for long enough if I started too soon!

As a teen, I became discouraged with the whole idea of living the Christian life. I grew increasingly aware of my total inability to live up to perfection. In fact, it seemed that I was getting worse. My body was developing, and I was struggling with new temptations. Much of the time I was failing to resist. I would respond whenever someone would make an appeal to seek God's forgiveness, but the next day I would fall back into old patterns of thinking and behavior. I felt that I was a total failure. No one ever told me that *grace* was a free gift and that my forgiveness was provided past, present and future in Jesus Christ. I thought my past was forgiven in Him, but I had to do the rest. I did not understand that when we are in a relationship with Jesus, His forgiveness is ours. He will change us. In the mean time, we are counted righteous at every step of the way. No one ever told me the good news. So I became increasingly discouraged and eventually gave up entirely on the Christian life. I decided that there was no hope for me. I was going to burn anyway, so I might as well go with class. I turned my back on God altogether and went into a season of complete rebellion.

During the next four years I did everything I could to self-destruct. As I look back on it now, I believe I had a death wish. I was so miserable. I spent those years getting high or drunk virtually non-stop. My hippie-type lifestyle had no boundaries. Yet I found no peace or rest from the

---

[5] Ellen G. White, *The Spirit of Prophecy*, Vol. 4, pp.307-315

pain. Several times I attempted suicide in my desperation or in times when drug supplies were low. Life was a dark blur of desperate, living hell. But God had not forsaken me. His love was greater than all my sin. I remember numerous times during those days when God appealed to me through people, events, dreams, and circumstances to draw me to Him.

One night in February of 1978, I was on a drug experience with one of my buddies, when we both began to think clearly. This was especially unusual since the drug known as "Angel Dust" commonly had the opposite effect. That night we both started talking about God and our own spiritual hunger. We saw our lives as they truly were, lost and broken. We realized that our lives were on a dangerous trajectory with only death or destruction awaiting us. We decided that night, with tears streaming down our faces, that we were going to join a "Jesus freak" commune just out of Los Angeles, California, and try to find the Lord. What I did not know at the time was that I had invited Jesus into my life. Instead of running away from Him, I had started walking toward Him. Jesus started a transformation in my life that is nothing short of miraculous. I soon found myself in a Christian recovery center called *The Bridge Fellowship* in Kentucky. For seven months I grew in the Word and in relationship with Jesus. I fell in love with the One who loved me first. I had personally experienced *grace*! For the first time in my life I began to understand what it meant to be a Christian. I had passed from death into life. My life would never be the same again. I will always be grateful to God for His amazing grace!

While at the recovery center, I started reading God's Word for myself, not just for a class assignment as I had done growing up. I began growing as a Christian as well as getting clean (sober). Those were wonderful days as I developed a personal walk with Jesus and learned about His personal love for me. I determined at that time that I was going to be a Christian, but I would never become an

Adventist again. My name had never been taken off of the church books, but I did not consider myself an SDA. I just wanted to be a believer in Jesus. I had felt so lost and so trapped by the legalism of my childhood and private high school days that I could not bear the thought of going back into that. I was a Christian now, and that was enough for me.

CHAPTER THREE

ADVENTIST EDUCATION AND MINISTRY

After seven months of reflection and renewal, however, the way was opened through my parents to go to Southern Adventist University (then known as Southern Missionary College, or affectionately in SDA circles as just Southern). The opportunity to go to college was appealing to me, and I wanted to make a fresh start with some college education. I was convinced, however, that I would not return to Adventism. I went there as a Christian wary of the denomination but anxious to learn about God. I was interested in training so that I could share the good news with others. I became involved with the student ministry opportunities on campus at Southern and found many Christian friends. I met several other new Christians who had been through experiences similar to my own. We were all on fire for Jesus and excited about taking the opportunity to share the good news with our friends on the campus. Many of these friends were SDA but had no relationship with Jesus. We found a field ripe for harvest. A grace awakening began to sweep that campus. I had the opportunity to be part of it.

The Adventist Church was experiencing a grace awakening on other college campuses as well. Adventist ministers such as Desmond Ford, Smuts van Rooyen, Morris Venden and many others, began boldly teaching the message of grace. Lives began to change, and the Gospel was proclaimed. Our own professors in the religion department at Southern were clearly teaching the good news to the students. Spiritual life began to spring up everywhere. They began to teach differently about the judgment and Law. While they did not repudiate SDA teachings, they approached them from a grace orientation. They still taught the seventh-day Sabbath, the investigative judgment and other core SDA doctrines, but focused on grace rather than legalism. They emphasized Ellen White's grace oriented statements instead of her legalistic, perfectionistic ones. I was blessed by these men as they shared God's love. It was at Southern that I became an Adventist by conviction.

I studied education because of a growing passion within me to teach in a church high school and help others in the Adventist system to learn about Jesus, rather than focus entirely on the legalistic rules of the church. I felt it was my personal mission to take the good news to youth and young adults who had been brought up in Christ-less legalism as I had been. I became active in youth ministry in one of the area churches and shared Jesus at every opportunity. By the time I was a senior, the local SDA conference (a regional association of Adventist churches with elected officers) sought me out and invited me to become a pastor. By this time, I was willing to consider serving in that role, something I had sensed God leading me to from my childhood but had resisted through most of my college experience. I accepted the invitation and served as an intern for one year at one of the local churches.

Meanwhile, Desmond Ford, a professor at Pacific Union College in California, released his research revealing that the investigative judgment doctrine was, in his estimation, not supportable by Scripture. He had been so captivated by the Gospel that he began to see that the idea of a judgment of believers that could cause them to lose their salvation ran contrary to the New Testament. He also pointed out that he believed the textual evidence in the Old Testament was insufficient to support such a doctrine. This caused a tidal wave of reaction in the church. The joy of the Gospel and the revival sweeping through the SDA church came under heavy resistance. The traditional wing of the church began to call the grace approach "new theology." It started resisting the message of *grace alone* as the only means to salvation. Desmond Ford was terminated from his position. Numerous other ministers and denominational workers were either terminated or resigned during the theological crisis. By the time I started in my new ministry position, there was an all out theological war raging at Southern Missionary College (Southern). The church where I ministered was just a few miles away, and we found ourselves in the midst of the controversy.

About the this time a book was released by another former SDA minister named Walter Rea, who had been a deep student of Ellen G. White. He was working on a companion volume to the Bible that would have quotations from the "spirit of prophecy" alongside the relevant texts of Scripture. This way, devoted Adventist readers would have the inspired commentary conveniently available as they would study the Bible. During his research, he visited Ellen White's residence at Elmshaven, her residence during her final years of life. He wanted to "get into the mind" of the woman that had so influenced generations of SDAs. He wanted to understand the author better so he could better reflect her thinking.

He found her library there and thought it would be interesting to see what kind of books she read for her personal use. He started reading some of them, and to his surprise and confusion, he found that much of the material in her writings had come directly out of these books without appropriate credit being given to any of the authors. In fact, at times Ellen White would describe what she was seeing in vision, or what she had been told by the angel, by using what she read, word for word, out of these books. He immediately contacted the White Estate of the General Conference of Seventh-day Adventists, and to his amazement they were not at all interested in his findings. In fact, they warned him to keep these things to himself or be fired. However, he continued to release his information and was, therefore, relieved of his position as a Seventh-day Adventist minister. Shortly thereafter he released his findings in a book titled, *The White Lie*.[1]

This was the backdrop to my first year in ministry. While traditional Adventists were pushing a legalistic perfectionism, others were taking their understanding of grace to its logical conclusion, rejecting the investigative judgment and the authority of Ellen White. Since Ellen White had so strongly taught the investigative judgment, declaring it to be the truth as she had seen it in vision, that very discussion destroyed the credibility of the Adventist prophet. The release of Walter Rea's materials revealed that there were many more issues to be considered. Could it be that Ellen White was not inspired as people had thought? By the end of that year, as I headed for the seminary at Andrews University, I seriously wondered if I was truly a Seventh-day Adventist. Shortly thereafter, my senior pastor was asked to resign, and many of the professors at Southern Missionary College were asked to resign or relocate.

During that year of chaos, several things happened in both my thinking and in my life. I had studied like never before. I had seen Adventism from a whole new perspective. One thing was clear; I knew from my own research in the manuscript documents that Ellen G. White definitely borrowed extensively from other authors and often attached the "I was shown" phrase to her writings. I also realized that the doctrine of the investigative judgment had serious flaws. So, with my new wife of 18 months, I went to Andrews Theological Seminary in Berrien Springs, Michigan, knowing that

[1] Walter Rea, *The White Lie*, (Turlock CA: M + R Publications, 1982)

I was in a precarious position as far as my belief regarding the church was concerned.

Several things happened to me at Andrews University that saved me for the SDA ministry. First, several of the professors poured grace into me. I flourished under this teaching. These men helped me see that the perfectionist mentality of those in the church who opposed Desmond Ford was not the position of all professors. Next, I was able to study the investigative judgment. I was given a few plausible explanations which at the time quieted my concerns. I know now that these solutions were grossly inadequate, but they were helpful at the time. What is more, some experts from the White Estate came to the campus with a lawyer's opinion that exonerated Ellen G. White of legal culpability in the plagiarism charges. I know today that this was only because of the legal loopholes in the law of her day. While I knew her plagiarism was illegal and wrong, the lawyer's report temporarily quieted my thinking.

The final and most important experience was that my wife, after a little over two years of marriage, decided that she was no longer interested in being married. When she left just before the midterm exams of the winter quarter, my main focus for the next year and a half was to survive. I put aside the theological issues of the day to focus on my own grieving process. However, my confidence in Ellen G. White was shaken and would never be the same again. While I knew that there were severe problems with her authority, I continued to read *The Desire of Ages* and *Steps to Christ*. I knew that to use her as a biblical commentary on a level with Scripture was to ignore the problems with her credibility.

During the grieving process I concentrated on the Word and my relationship with Jesus. Only those who have experienced divorce can comprehend the pain. The sense of personal rejection and failure drove me to Jesus as never before. Theological discussion had its place, but my heart needed the comfort and healing available only through time spent with my Lord. Because of the obvious choices my ex-wife made, I was permitted to maintain my seminary sponsorship and ministry assignments (part-time while at Seminary).

While at Andrews I made the acquaintance of a pretty young communications student named Paula Wesner. We became well acquainted through campus ministry activities. While we never dated until after I graduated from the seminary, we enjoyed long conversations and developed a lasting and meaningful friendship. Upon leaving Andrews our friendship developed into a long-distance relationship and finally marriage in March of 1985. Paula has been my loving wife and faithful partner in ministry ever since.

Paula and I dedicated ourselves to the Seventh-day Adventist ministry. At first we pastored in a couple of districts where I was a circuit riding pastor. We held regular evangelistic meetings, *Revelation seminars*, and other outreach events as requested by our conference. I loved the preaching/teaching side of ministry and the relationship development. I loved helping people come to Jesus. But I became increasingly uncomfortable with the traditional evangelistic methods. It was expected that ministers hold a "crusade" at least once each year, especially if they had not yet been ordained. I needed to prove my calling to ministry by effective "evangelism." But the focus on last-day events and prophetic interpretation was clearly targeted at the individual already attending some other church. This felt more like proselytism than evangelism to me. It was an effort to win Christians from other churches into Adventism so that they would become part of the "remnant" church. This emphasis felt wrong to me. I felt my calling was to reach people with the Gospel of Jesus Christ, to lead them to Him as their Savior, and help them learn to live in relationship with Him. Traditional Adventist evangelistic meetings dedicated only one or two nights to the Gospel, and the rest to their distinctive doctrines. I felt much of the methodology of concealing the SDA name and using a public hall was deceptive. Much of the content of the seminars was based on proof texts that I knew were suspect. They were not supported by context. I eventually became frustrated with the district pastorate. I was uncomfortable with what appeared to me to be evangelism by proselytism and a ministry too focused on Adventism versus Christianity. When an opportunity arose for me to be a full-time youth pastor, I accepted it without hesitation. We went to Kettering, Ohio, where I served the youth of the Kettering SDA Church for six and a half years.

Paula is a natural at hospitality, and I love sharing basic Christianity with others. It was a perfect match. We were far removed from the theological issues of the day and right into the important ministry of leading young people to Jesus. Most of them had, like me, been raised in the SDA Church, but did not know Jesus. I shared the good news of salvation with them and had the privilege of leading many of them into a saving relationship with the Lord. Paula provided a warm and hospitable environment for this to take place. We saw many young people come to Christ and some go into full-time ministry.

During this time, however, I neglected to balance ministry with personal life and did not take enough private time to rejuvenate. Youth ministry is extremely time-consuming. Planning all week and leading events all weekend (often into the wee hours of the morning) took their toll. I almost burned out. We decided we needed to leave youth ministry at that time. We began to pray for another opportunity to serve in general church ministry. I needed time to learn how to walk closer to Jesus and to make seeking Him top priority. I had allowed myself to get so busy with the "work of the Lord" that I had little time for the "Lord of the work." Thanks to God and to a few good friends, I was nurtured back to health and experienced another breakthrough in my spiritual life, much like a new conversion of a much deeper nature.

Paula was also growing, and not just spiritually! She became pregnant with our first son, Jordan. A few years later

Matthew also arrived. These very special gifts from God have helped us understand God's love in an entirely new and deeper way. God's grace is so amazing! Along with children came the realization that we could not keep up with the youth ministry and remain balanced. We had a family of our own now to care for. We also had a deep sense that God was calling us to something special. One day an invitation came for us to go to Asheville, North Carolina.

CHAPTER FOUR

THE HUNGER FOR MORE

In Asheville, we found a church that was trying to transition to more contemporary methods of outreach. They were using youth ministry principles, as well as methods used by the Willow Creek Community Church in Chicago, to reach adults for Jesus. We prayed much about the decision, because we were well aware of the dangers of trying to transition a church to a more contemporary model. While Asheville would be a delightful place to live, the ministry risks would be high. Many have tried to lead transitions, but few have succeeded. So we prayed earnestly for God's guidance. After many clear indications of His providence, we moved to North Carolina.

Our new ministry began an intense yet rewarding period in our lives. Tremendous personal and spiritual growth took place within us, and God blessed our church. In spite of the fact that some 50 people left during the transition from a traditional to a contemporary model, the church grew from an average attendance of 120 before the transition to a vibrant congregation of 500 members and an attendance that nearly tripled. We saw the hand of the Lord in the renewal at the Foster Memorial Church.[1] My evangelism gift was able to function in a way that enabled me to use non-traditional methods of ministry. Paula was able to use her gifts of hospitality and creative communication, and our boys were able to enjoy many friends and a great community. Foster Memorial Church was truly an evangelical church within the SDA system. We were delighted to help many free themselves from the legalism of their youth and enjoy an assurance of their salvation in Jesus Christ.

During this time we visited Willow Creek Community Church, a highly recognized interdenominational church in Chicago, Illinois, for numerous training events. We were privileged to connect with other Christians who love Jesus and are sold out to reaching the world for Him. My heart for evangelism burned within me as I caught a vision of what church could be. I saw that an Acts Two church was possible in our generation. I knew that I had to give my life to reaching truly lost people. I could not be satisfied with a church that grew solely by drawing people from other churches. There are so many people who do not know Jesus, that to engage in turf wars is an unacceptable waste of time and of God's resources.

It was at Willow Creek that we were introduced to contemporary worship. We had never before experienced real worship. Yes, we had private time with God, but to meet with a body of believers and sing praises *to* God, instead of songs *about* Him, was a life-changing experience for us. The worship times at Willow Creek reflected a taste of heaven for us. I remember discussing how worship in this place was so much more vibrant than anything we had ever experienced in Adventism. I remember thinking and discussing with Paula that the remnant people of God will be people with a passion for reaching the lost and who love

---

[1] The Foster Memorial Church is a Seventh-day Adventist church in Asheville, North Carolina.

worship. That is the message of the first angel of Revelation 14:6-7. We had a deep desire to see these things happen in our own local church. We tried to share much of what we learned at Willow Creek with the membership of Foster Memorial Church. Gradually God led us as a church to a more open and expressive style of worship and a deeper commitment to reaching lost people.

For a long time I had a problem with the idea that the Adventists were the one and only remnant church. I felt that the focus was too small and believed the concept of a remnant message rather than that of a "remnant church" was a more realistic interpretation of Revelation 12. The problem of the lack of spiritual renewal in most SDA churches and the presence of abundant life in non-SDA churches was of continuing concern to me.

After about five years, we started seeing a leveling off in growth at Foster Memorial Church. Although still a vibrant church, it seemed that its witness was failing to reach our target group, the unchurched people around us. Those we did reach usually had some form of Adventist background. While this is an important group to reach with the Gospel, it was, for the most part, the only group we were reaching. I prayed intently about this concern. My evangelism gift was burning inside me, yet it seemed that something was blocking its effectiveness. I began to think that there must be something wrong with me. I spent much time in soul searching. Is this just an ego problem that makes me long for a large church, or is it the passion for lost people that is driving me? I went for some Christian counseling, which proved most helpful, not only in solving the issues of success and failure that I was dealing with, but also with some issues from my past about which I was less aware. I was able to look at the parts of me that needed healing, confess them to the Lord and receive His forgiveness.

Meanwhile, the church remained plateaued. I found that I was not as interested in the size of the church as I was in using the evangelistic gifts God had given me. This was a time of deep soul-searching. I knew something was blocking God's plan for using this gift in my life, but I didn't know what it was. We explored a few calls, but did not sense the Lord leading us away at that time. I would go away for spiritual retreats of fasting and prayer to ask God for direction. I claimed Luke 11:11-13 for the presence of the Holy Spirit and for clear direction from God.

About this time a friend in a similar ministry invited Carl George, an outreach and church growth specialist, to come and assess his church because its growth had also plateaued. Carl George's assessment of this church was that it could not break into the unchurched community because of the Sabbath issues, which posed too great a barrier for most people unfamiliar with Adventism. For pastors called to reach unchurched people for Jesus, this seemed an insurmountable problem. We must reach the world, yet we are encountering a barrier that is a part of the very structure of Adventism. At this point, I decided to trust God and accept that if He wanted to use us to reach people outside the system, He would make it happen.

Meanwhile, two of my friends, Richard Fredericks and Clay Peck, who had been pastoring in similar ministries, left Adventism to start non-denominational churches. Their initial separation from the SDA Church was a result of financial issues between themselves and the conferences they served. They were struggling to support a full church ministry while at the same time sending 100% of their tithe away to the conference. This issue is one that every Adventist pastor faces. Adventist Churches are required to send all tithe monies to the parent organization, which in turn provides pastoral salaries through the organization. All the local ministry expenses must be met from monies donated beyond tithe. Because of this, a significant administrative hierarchy has developed, leaving many local churches in the Adventist system financially crippled. The local church is often lost sight of in the denominational structure. Only about 30-33% of the tithe dollars actually go for pastoral salaries, and of those, many are administrative rather than pastoral. A full 40% of tithe in the Adventist Church goes to support its massive educational system.[2] I was sympathetic with my friends' situation because they had tried repeatedly to work out a more equitable funding arrangement with the church system and had been repeatedly denied.

However, soon after they moved out of the Adventist system they began to examine the seventh-day Sabbath. After some extensive study they concluded that the seventh-day Sabbath was not required in the New Covenant, and they transitioned to a Sunday worship format. I must admit that at the time I was angry with them. I felt they had caused a dark cloud over the already shaky contemporary evangelism movement within the church. I felt that the evangelical wing of the church would suffer because of their actions. I had been much less concerned when they left the church over issues with the tithe, since the SDA system does severely strangle the local church of its resources. Adventist pastors from the most conservative to the most progressive experience these problems. I had hoped that Richard Fredericks and Clay Peck would prove that Sabbath-keeping churches outside the umbrella of the SDA system could be financially viable and successful. But the Sabbath issue discredited them in my view and in that of most of the SDA Church community. I told them how I felt. They were both gracious enough to listen to my concerns, share some of their ideas with me, and behaved towards me as Christian gentlemen.

When these pastor friends left Adventism and later the Sabbath, I went through a time of study. My primary reason for being an Adventist was the Sabbath. I had believed up to that point that the Seventh-day Adventist Church came

---

[2] Greg Taylor, "Stop Strangling the Goose", *Adventist Today*, Vol. 9, issue 3, May-June 2001, pp. 14-15.

the closest to teaching Bible truth of any church I had ever encountered. In this respect, I was solidly Adventist by conviction, in spite of my concerns regarding Ellen White, the investigative judgment and the remnant church teachings. I was convinced that Sabbath was God's special day. My sermons during this time were clearly direct on this issue. I also taught new believers that while Adventism was not a perfect church, it was the closest to biblical truth as I understood it. Therefore, I had no problem calling people to make a commitment to become members of the Adventist Church. I would often continue by stating that if I ever discovered greater truth in the Bible I would follow it. I felt that the Sabbath was so solidly biblical that it made the other problems of less concern.

I studied the materials that my friends Richard and Clay, who had left the denomination, recommended. I also poured over materials written by Adventist theologians, including Samuel Bacchiocchi, the Church's foremost authority on the Sabbath. In addition, I consulted two of the denomination's most respected professors and writers. My passion was to prove where my friends were wrong. I read, studied and convinced myself that the Adventists have the truth on the Sabbath. I also believed Ellen G. White had the spiritual gift of prophecy even though she was not reliable as an interpreter of Scripture. I saw Adventists as having a remnant message, although not exclusively. The 1844 investigative judgment, though complicated, could be made to agree with Ellen White's position, with some creative imagination and proof-texts. But the kingpin for me was the seventh-day Sabbath, for with no seventh-day Sabbath there can be no Seventh-day Adventist Church.

About this time my family and I were preparing to start on a Sabbatical. We had planned to travel around the USA and see national parks and on the weekends visit churches. That is just what we did. We had a wonderful trip. All along the way we asked the Lord to show us what He wanted us to do with our lives. We wanted to be open to

His leadership and follow Him no matter what the cost. Having a whole summer to study, pray, listen and observe seemed like a great way to hear God's voice. It was a wonderful summer. I would pray and listen each day. Each time I sensed the Lord telling me to just wait. God let me know through prayer and deep study that what He wanted me to learn from the sabbatical experience would hit me all at once, and it would be biblical and crystal clear.

During the summer we were struck with the lack of spiritual vitality in all of the Adventist Churches we visited. While the people were sincere, there was such a dearth of life that it was depressing. It was almost as if they were just going through the motions of "doing church." The Sunday churches were the other way around. With the exception of one church we visited, all of them had such life and joy that it was contagious. We would rejoice when we attended churches of various denominations or independent communities. Then as we visited the SDA churches, we would become sad and depressed. I remember praying, "Why Lord, if the Sabbath is so significant a part of Your moral law and binding on all Christians, are You clearly blessing other churches, while the Adventist Churches are, at best, just maintaining?" We came back from our sabbatical both energized and saddened. We were so happy to get back into our church where there was much vibrancy. Before I went back to work I spent three days alone on a spiritual retreat studying and praying for God's leading for the next season of ministry. I wrote in my journal, studied, prayed and reflected. Still the same answer, "You will know what I have for you to learn, and it will be soon. I have a plan for your life and will reveal it through My Word."

Nothing could have prepared me for what happened next. I received a call from a fellow Adventist pastor and long-time friend who I knew to be in love with Jesus like few others in my life. I have great respect for his walk with the Lord and commitment to following Him no matter the cost. He opened up to me and shared that he had been studying the Sabbath and was not sure that the SDA position was biblically sound and in accord with the New Testament. This blew me away to say the least. My friend mentioned the same observations I had concerning the non-sabbatarian churches having such an obvious anointing of the Spirit of God while SDA churches were struggling. I shared with him my struggles with this question. To make a long story short, several other friends who I know to be sold out to Jesus were all simultaneously dealing with the same issues. That began an intense time of study for me. I went back to the materials I had studied to argue with my former Adventist colleagues, and this time I decided to study them with an open Bible and an open mind. Perhaps God was trying to tell me something. Each day I claimed God's promise in Luke 11:11-13 as I studied the Word. I learned to trust that when I ask for the guidance of the Holy Spirit, God would send Him to me, and that He would not instead give me a stone, a snake, or a scorpion. I decided to trust God's Word and believe that He would guide my wife and me into all truth. He would not allow us to be deceived if we earnestly asked Him for guidance.

Let me say one more thing. The study of the Sabbath, because of my position as an Adventist pastor, carried enormous personal risk. Everything I have ever known as a Christian and a minister could be at risk. My wife also had deep connections in the church. We had life-long friendships that we held dear. We had a church that we loved dearly and that loved us. We had no particular, marketable skills outside of ministry. Paula had put her writing career on hold so she could be at home with our sons. We had no careers to fall back on in an emergency. So it was with fear and trepidation that we started to study, not knowing what might come of it. From the bottom of our hearts we wanted to follow the Lord, even if it meant losing everything. After all, we had encouraged people through the years to follow God no matter the cost and trust Him with the results. What kind of spiritual leaders would we be if we refused to risk all for the cause of Christ ourselves?

What we learned from God's Word literally upset and radically transformed our world. At the same time, it has been the most liberating and soul satisfying study we have ever embarked on. True to His promise, God completely rearranged our way of thinking. We have come to an understanding of the Bible in a whole new and powerful way. It has cost us our position as senior pastor in a large Adventist Church. We have lost the respect of many we once served. We have lost the security of a 20-year career (18+ years of which were full-time). But we have gained a depth of closeness with the Spirit and joy in our walk with God that cannot be compared with the little we lost. God has been more than faithful to us. There is not a day that goes by that we do not thank God for allowing us to understand his amazing New Covenant of grace.

You may remember some years ago there was a "Hidden Picture" craze. These "Magic Eye" pictures, as they were called, showed up in offices, books, lobbies, etc. Often crowds of people gathered around these pictures, which appeared at first glance to be nothing more than a mixture of colors randomly splashed across the page. But as people would concentrate on these works of art, one after another would exclaim loudly, "I see it! I see it!" Then they would immediately coach others on the correct way to look at the painting so they could see it too. I did my share of staring at these pictures. I wanted to see what was so exciting in these otherwise strange looking paintings. But I was not one of the fortunate ones. I saw nothing.

Then one day, with some time to kill, I sat down in front of one of these wall-hung versions and just stared. It must have been 15-20 minutes that I sat there just staring. I was just about to give up and call the whole thing a farce when all at once I saw it! A beautiful three dimensional rendition of the Statue of Liberty seemed to jump off of the canvas. It was truly amazing! I could hardly believe it.

Soon I was leafing through a book of similar paintings looking for their hidden secrets. What a discovery! Once I made that initial discovery, all of the pictures seemed to come alive. I could never look at one of these hidden pictures in the same way again.

In much the same way, the Scriptures came to life for Paula and me as we studied. At first we saw what we had always seen. Then one day they came to life for us. We begin to see the Bible as we had never seen it before. After seeing the truth come to life, we could never view the Bible in the same way again. We do not in any way want to put down another person's understanding of Scripture. Nor do we want to say that we are right and others are wrong. All we can say is that we have seen a picture of God and His Word that has shattered all our previous paradigms and given us a new and more complete understanding of God's gift to mankind. We are forever grateful for this gift of God's grace.

In the chapters that follow I will explain the theological process that God took us through to break free of the Adventist theological worldview.

CHAPTER FIVE

THE ISSUE OF ELLEN G. WHITE

Our first step of the journey had to be a decision on the ministry of Ellen G. White (EGW). Paula and I have taken the position that we are going to be "Bible and the Bible only" people. That does not mean that we do not consider there to be a proper place for spiritual gifts, but we are to test the gifts by the Word, and not the other way around. In our formation of theology, we must go to the Word.

We must make reference to the fact that there are severe problems with Ellen White's writings that, unfortunately, the Adventist Church has been unwilling to deal with openly. To be fair, we suggest that every concerned individual do some research on his or her own and decide what is the truth regarding Ellen White's claims. I suggest the internet as a means for researching Ellen White. Sites can be found that are pro-EGW and others that are critics of her ministry. One should read both to arrive at a fair conclusion. Remember that I Thessalonians 5:20-21 tells us not to despise prophesies, but to prove all things and hold fast to that which is good.

We have come to the conclusion from our research that she is not a reliable prophetic voice. That does not mean that

Ellen White was not inspirational at times. We both love the books *Steps to Christ* and *The Desire of Ages,* which are wonderful books about the Christian life and the life of Jesus Christ respectively. But she clearly, knowingly and extensively copied from other sources while claiming that she was not doing so except in a few rare cases. Some estimates of her borrowing are as high as 90%.[1] Even the *Desire of Ages*, my favorite EGW book has, according to a church sponsored study, "no significant line of thinking that is original"[2] to her. The study goes on to admit that this issue "strikes at the heart of her honesty, integrity and therefore her trustworthiness."[3] Even in her works where she said "I was shown," there is evidence of extensive copying. She copied down materials from other authors and in many cases included the errors right along with the truth.[4]

Some have said that the laws were different back then. She could not have been convicted in a court of law in her day. Maybe not, but both James and Ellen White were quite adamant that others should not borrow from them without giving credit! They even took others to task who had done so, pointing out the dishonesty of the practice.[5] The community feeling regarding literary piracy was much the same. I have in my possession a copy of the Healdsburg newspaper dated March 20, 1889, where the local community was upset over the discovery of some significant plagiarism in her writings. The practice of literary borrowing without giving credit was plainly not acceptable in her day. Clearly it was dishonest and she knew it. The people in her

---

[1] Walter Rea, *How the Seventh-day Adventist Spirit of Prophecy Was Born*, p. 1

[2] Fred Veltman, "*The Desire of Ages Project*: The Conclusions," *Ministry*, 1990, p. 11.

[3] Ibid. p 14.

[4] Maurice Barnett, *Ellen G. White and Inspiration* (Beaumont, TX: The Preceptor Co. 1983) p. 37-47.

[5] Ibid. p. 38-39

own neighborhood did not approve of it. It was this discovery that forced her to admit using outside sources in the book *The Great Controversy*. Even then, she only admitted what she knew others knew about her use of sources. It is not wrong to use source material. But Ellen White was careful to point out to others that proper credit must always be given when using material from another author. Meanwhile she was disregarding these guidelines in her own work. She was claiming originality in her writings. This double standard is deeply problematic.[6] The Scriptures make it plain that such dishonest borrowing is not pleasing to the Lord. Notice Jeremiah 23:30.

> "Therefore behold, I am *against the prophets*," says the LORD, "*who steal My words every one from his neighbor.*"

There is also the cover up of her visions that taught the opposite of what she later believed. *Early Writings* claims in the preface pages iii and iv that there have been no deletions. They claim to include all of her early works. They claim that only a word here and there has been substituted to update the original meaning. All of this was done "under the author's own approval." The truth is, significant portions of her early visions were left out, and the original meaning was changed. I have seen comparisons between her earlier documents and the book *Early Writings*. Clearly the deletions were

---

[6] Ellen White wrote to Jones and Waggoner in 1887, "I have not been in the habit of reading any doctrinal articles in the paper, that my mind should not have any understanding of anyone's views, and that not a mold of any man's theories should have any connection with that which I write." Letter 37-1887. She also wrote in 1904, "I am glad you are having success in selling my books; for thus you are giving to the world the light that God has given me. These books contain clear, straight, unalterable truth and they should certainly be appreciated. The instruction they contain is not of human production." Letter 339-1904.

intentional and misleading.[7] EGW knew full well what was going on. These suppressed writings have been covered up by the church and by EGW herself.

There are many more problems, however. I will just touch on a very few. One is the issue of her failed predictions. During the Civil War, Ellen White predicted that England would join the South and declare war on the North. This would cause the tide to turn in the conflict and would enable the Confederacy to win the war.[8] American history clearly proves that this was not true. She also prophesied that, according to her visions, Old Jerusalem would never be rebuilt.[9] Here again history has proven that her prediction was not inspired. Since the rebirth of the nation of Israel in 1948, old Jerusalem has been greatly rebuilt. On one occasion, in May of 1856, she was addressing a group of Adventists and made the statement that some of these people would die, some would receive the seven last plagues and others would be alive at Jesus' return.[10] Everyone who was

---

[7] One example can be seen in the difference between *The Remnant Scattered Abroad* and the book *Early Writings*. The original edition includes a sentence regarding the "Shut Door." Early Adventists believed that in 1844 the door of salvation to the world had been closed. Only Adventists that had believed and continued to believe in the 1844 message would be saved. Ellen White described what she saw in vision regarding those who had rejected this light. "It was just as impossible for them to get on the path again to go to the City, as all the wicked world which God had rejected. They fell all along the path one after another." Later Adventists would move away from this idea, but Ellen White had seen in vision that salvation was no longer available to those outside the Adventist family. What would they do? Instead of admitting the mistake, they deleted the problematic statements. Then they covered up the deletion as seen in the preface to *Early Writings*. Clearly more than a word was involved in this deletion. The editors actually changed the meaning of the original vision and attempted to cover up the author's former beliefs.

[8] Ellen G. White, *Testimonies for the Church*, Vol. 1, p 259.

[9] Ellen G. White, *Early Writings*, p. 75.

[10] Ellen G. White, *Testimonies for the Church*, Vol. 1, pp. 131-132.

in attendance at that meeting has been dead for many years. Once again her predictions fail the test of time. There are many more examples of this failure. What are we to make of such discrepancies? The Bible tells us that we are to test the prophetic voice, not only by the fruit of the ministry (Matt 7:20) and the truth of the Gospel (Gal.1:8-9), but by their predictions. Deuteronomy 18:20-22 says:

> And if you say in your heart, "How shall we know the word which the LORD has not spoken?"-- when a prophet speaks in the name of the LORD, if the thing does not happen or come to pass, that is the thing which the LORD has not spoken; the prophet has spoken it presumptuously; you shall not be afraid of him.

Ellen White made other statements in her "prophetic role" that reflected the ideas of her time and not divine inspiration at all. She stated that wearing wigs can cause a person to become reckless in morals.[11] She taught that tight lacing of corsets causes defective body shape and breathing in women and this is passed along to their children.[12] She also taught that this practice could cause the lungs to protrude out of the neck.[13] She stated that babies who nurse from a wet nurse will inherit that woman's morals.[14] She also reflected the misinformed thinking of some in her day in such issues as science and social mores. This included racial prejudices. She stated that certain races of men are the result of the amalgamation of man and beast.[15]

Her writings do not seem to reflect the balance of the Scriptures either. For example, she mentions Sabbath in her

---

[11] Ellen G. White, *Healthful Living*, p. 1851
[12] Ellen G. White, *Health Reformer*, 1871-11-01
[13] Ibid. 1871-10-31
[14] Ellen G. White, *Healthful Living*, p. 145
[15] Ellen G. White, *Spiritual Gifts*, Vol. 3, p. 75

writings some 3,315 times while the Bible does so in only 116 verses. She mentions Satan 9,956 times when the Bible does so only 47 times. She repeatedly mentions the frown of God or the frown of Christ, and usually in the context of herself or some other believer who was not measuring up to perfection. She talks about this frown some 147 times.[16] These examples alone indicate a lack of balance in her writings.

For us, the biggest problem with Ellen White is the effect she has had on the SDA Church. There is still wide misunderstanding of the Gospel of grace in Adventism. In our years of service this has been an enormous barrier in helping people find assurance. It is not that she did not teach grace. She did teach it beautifully at times, but she also taught perfectionism. Adventists are still basically confused as a people about the very core of the Christian faith. It is so difficult for most Adventists to grasp the Gospel because of these statements. We have never seen an Adventist Church truly dedicated to applying the writings of EGW that is a vibrant, alive, growing, happy church community. The responsibility for this falls directly on the shoulders of EGW. Surely a church with 100,000 pages of "inspired" writings should have an even greater grasp on the Good News than other churches. Sadly, this is not the case. Jesus teaches us to test the prophets by their fruits. What do we do with the problems just mentioned? Galatians 1:8 states that even if an "angel of light" comes and teaches a different Gospel, let him be accursed. Ellen White did not teach a "faith that works" but a "faith plus works" theology.[17] She was opposed to anyone using the phrase "I am saved." She said, "No sanctified tongue will be found uttering these words till Christ shall come, and we enter in through the gates into the

---

[16] Dale Ratzlaff, *The Cultic Doctrine of Seventh-day Adventists*, (Life Assurance Ministries, 1998) p. 294

[17] Ellen G. White, *Sketches from the Life of Paul*, p. 192.

city of God."[18] "As long as man is full of weakness—for himself he cannot save his soul—he should never dare to say 'I am saved' "[19] Even in some of her later works, such as *The Great Controversy*, this perfectionism is still present. Read the chapter on the investigative judgment entitled *Facing Life's Record* and see what you think. With just these issues alone we are compelled to say that Ellen White is, at best, unreliable as a prophet. We surely cannot say that we should take her opinions as a companion volume to the Bible.

We believe there are some key reasons why it is hard to let the full truth about EGW come out. One key reason may be the identity issue within the church. Adventists have a vested interest in preserving their claim that EGW was a true prophet on the scale of one of the biblical prophets. It is part of the "remnant church" identity. The decision of the Bible Conference held in 1919 by the General Conference was that there should be an immediate disclosure of the problems with Ellen White as a prophetic voice in the church. The amount of material copied and the attempts to hide the facts was considered by her long-time fellow laborer, W. W. Prescott and others, to be dishonest and deceptive.[20]

Prompted by the discovery that the book *Life Sketches from the Life of Paul* had been borrowed almost in its entirety, and without recognition, from a book by Coneybeare and Howson,[21] they attempted to help people under-

---

[18] Ellen G. White, *The Kress Collection*, p. 120.
[19] Ellen G. White, *Bible Echo*, 1897-02-08.
[20] Desmond Ford, *Daniel 8:14* (Newcastle California, Ford Publications, 1980) p. 370.
[21] Sydney Cleveland, *White Washed*, (Glendale Arizona, Life Assurance Ministries, 2000) p. 12-22. The official minutes of the 1919 Bible conference were discovered in a vault at the General Conference headquarters in 1974. The documents had been intentionally sealed with instructions that they were not to be opened for 50 years! The leaders had knowingly covered up the issues with Ellen Whites plagarism rather then face the disappointment and backlash of the membership in the church. So the myths about Ellen White continued.

stand the truth about her gift. But there was such a backlash against those who were trying to clarify the truth, that some key Bible teachers were terminated. Unfortunately, the denomination stepped away from disclosing the full truth about Ellen G. White. An atmosphere of fear to discuss these issues prevailed. Today, Adventists have to face this reality after many more years of ingrained misconceptions.

The Revelation 12:17 statement that the remnant will keep the commandments of God (which SDAs take to mean the Ten Commandments) is part of this remnant identity in the church. The second part of the passage states that this "remnant" will have the testimony of Jesus. The Adventists then teach that the Revelation 19:10 statement, "The testimony of Jesus is the spirit of prophecy," indicates that the testimony of Jesus and the prophetic gift are one and the same. Thus they conclude that the "true church" of the last days will teach all of God's commandments, including the fourth, and will have a prophet. Many SDAs affectionately call the writings of Ellen White the "Spirit of Prophecy."

The problem with this interpretation is that it does injustice to the linguistics and to the context of Revelation. In Revelation 19:10, the "spirit of prophecy" is a clear reference to the Holy Spirit. It is another name for the Holy Spirit that inspired the prophets. This same Spirit is behind all proclamation of the Gospel. To interpret that the testimony of Jesus always refers to the prophetic voice would be to ignore what the rest of Revelation says about the testimony of Jesus. For example, in Revelation 1:2 it says that John "bore witness to the word of God and to the testimony of Jesus Christ, and to all things that he saw." This was clearly not a reference to the prophetic gift. He certainly was not making a reference to Ellen White. In context, it appears to be a reference to the Gospel message. Now notice verse 9. Here, John says he was on the Isle of Patmos for "the word of God and the testimony of Jesus Christ." Does this refer to the prophetic gift? No, it is not even a reference to prophecy in general. He had not yet received any prophetic visions. This is a clear reference to the Gospel, the testimony (witness) about Jesus. It became clear to me that to fit Ellen White into Revelation 12:17 was a stretch as well. I do not want to be guilty of reading my own version of eschatology into the text rather than letting the text speak for itself. This is incredibly dangerous in light of the warnings about adding to or subtracting from the words of the book found in chapter 22:18-19.

During this time of study and reflection I went to a professor at the Adventist Theological Seminary who specialized in Ellen G. White. He gave me an afternoon to just talk. He was quite open with me as I plied him with questions. We talked about the massive copying that Mrs. White had done. He was well aware of her issues. His bottom line was that we cannot use her as a companion volume to the Bible and we cannot use her as an authority source for theology. He also admitted that the *Clear Word Bible* should never have been written. He had made his objections clear, but no one had listened to him. He said that Ellen White had herself told the brethren not to use her as an authority source when they were studying Galatians back in 1888. They should study the Word first. I then replied, "She should have said that when she knew that she had copied the entire book, *Sketches from the Life of Paul* from Coneybeare and Howson." He smiled at me and said nothing.

I then asked him, "Knowing all the problems with Ellen White, how can you go along with the church position that she is a 'continuing and authoritative source of truth'?" He told me that only applies to statements she made to individuals in personal prophecies and testimonies, and can only be applied to the church as a whole if we have the context. "The problem is," he continued, "we don't have the context for most of these personal prophetic statements in our source material." In other words, I knew that he did not buy into the church position at all. He, along with many other scholars, was trying to find a way to get around the problems rather than face the issues squarely. To question Ellen G. White is to lose one's job in the Adventist system.

I asked him about the many strange statements, the clear cover-ups, and other problems. He just said to me. "Greg, you have to look at the big picture. You are just looking at the problem areas. You have to focus on the main themes of what she said." With that our conversation came to an end. We had been together for some time and it was time for me to leave. But I kept pondering those words. They seemed to repeat themselves over and over again in my mind. The issues just did not go away. I began to ask myself, "If I was a Mormon and I was asking my leaders about the problems with Joseph Smith, the Mormon 'prophet', would they not be giving me the same response? Would I have the courage, if I were a Mormon, to face the truth about him? The pressures would be the same in that system. Would I have the courage to step out on my convictions if I were there?" As an Adventist, I had no problem seeing through the issues with Joseph Smith because I had no vested interest in having to believe in him. But I had a huge vested interest in trying to believe in the authority of Ellen White. My job and the livelihood of my family were at stake. Friendships, family ties, belief system, respect in the community in which I served, were all at stake here.

As I drove home, I contrasted the "big picture" approach to Ellen White's writings and her own statements about her authority. She forbids people from picking and choosing in her writings. She required total belief in her writings or total rejection. She did not allow for examination and questions regarding her authority. She condemned those who tried to "pick and choose" and decide which things were in agreement with Scripture and which were not.[22] She stated the she had not written any heretical statements in her

[22] Ellen G. White, *Testimonies for the Church*, Vol. 5, p. 691.

writings.[23] They were either all true or all from the devil.[24] She warned that those who began to question her authority as a prophet would eventually lose their belief in the Scriptures and lose their salvation.

> It is Satan's plan to weaken the faith of God's people in the *Testimonies.* Next follows skepticism in regard to the vital points of our faith, the pillars of our position, then doubt as to the Holy Scriptures and then the downward march to perdition.[25]

> Those who would in any way lessen the force of the sharp reproofs which God has given me to speak, must meet their work in the judgment.[26]

> The very last deception of Satan will be to make of none effect the testimony of the Spirit of God… Satan will work ingeniously, in different ways and through different agencies, to unsettle the confidence of God's remnant people in the true testimony.[27]

These are fear inducing words and certainly not the kind that invite questioning and examination as Paul required in proving the reliability of the prophetic word. In First Thessalonians 5:19-21 he makes it plain, "Do not quench the Spirit. Do not despise prophecies. *Test all things; hold fast what is good.*" (emphasis mine)

I shared these things with Paula when I arrived home. We prayed earnestly for God to give us courage to follow

---

[23] Ellen G. White, in a letter addressed to her granddaughter Mabel. Nov. 16, 1905.
[24] Ellen G. White, *Testimonies for the Church*, Vol. 4, p. 230.
[25] Ibid. Vol. 4, p. 211.
[26] Ibid. Vol. 5, p. 19.
[27] Ellen G. White, *Selected Messages*, Vol. 2, p. 78.

Him and truly test these things by His Word. Ellen White's statements were indeed frightening and caused us to call out to God for wisdom and direction like never before. Yet, as we put the pieces together, we were compelled to take the Bible and the Bible only in our study. We felt that any other course would not be taking the *biblical warnings* seriously. Even though Ellen White had written many wonderful words of truth, there were also many things that contradicted the Gospel, were clearly not inspired, and indicated dishonest literary practices. To continue to use her to interpret Scripture would be to ignore the biblical tests of a prophet and the warnings attached to doing so.

CHAPTER SIX

THE INVESTIGATIVE JUDGMENT

Another issue that we had to encounter was the unique Adventist doctrine, the investigative judgment. As mentioned earlier, this is the one doctrine, with the exception of the "prophetic" status given to Ellen White, that is held only and exclusively by Seventh-day Adventists. Other churches or individuals believe in the prophetic gift, soul sleep, and annihilation of the wicked versus an ever burning hell, the Levitical food laws, and Saturday Sabbath. None, however, to my knowledge believe in the investigative judgment. This does not necessarily mean that Adventists are incorrect. It does, however, send up some warning signals that there must be strong and unequivocal scriptural support for such a doctrine if it is to be considered the centerpiece of a denomination and a test of fellowship.

As stated in the first chapter, early Adventists were fascinated by Bible prophecy, especially the one in Daniel 8:13-14:

> Then I heard a holy one speaking, and another holy one said to him, "How long will it take for the vision to be fulfilled--the vision concerning the daily sacrifice, the rebellion that causes desolation, and the surrender of the sanctuary and of the host that will be trampled

underfoot?" He said to me, "It will take 2,300 evenings and mornings; then the sanctuary will be reconsecrated." (NIV)

William Miller had come to the conclusion that this was a reference to the second coming of Christ and therefore, Jesus would come in 1843. Connecting the start of the 2300 day prophecy with the start of the prophecy of the Messiah in Daniel 9, the command to restore and rebuild Jerusalem, had given him a starting point. While most scholars today do not agree with the starting point he chose because it was not the right command for restoration and rebuilding, Miller nevertheless convinced many thousands of people, especially in New England, that Jesus would come by the end of 1843. He later changed this to 1844 because of the absence of a year "Zero" between BC and AD in historical reckoning. There were three disappointments. The first came when Jesus did not return in 1843, the second when the spring of 1844 passed, and most importantly the final and Great Disappointment of October 22, 1844. This last date had come to the forefront because of the connection of the cleansing of the sanctuary with the Day of Atonement in the Jewish calendar and described in Leviticus 16.

This disappointment was devastating to the early Adventists. Many of them had not harvested crops and had burned relationships with their former churches by calling them "Babylon" and "Apostate."[1] Many Adventists had been expelled from their churches, not because their fellow Christians did not believe that the second coming of Christ was near, but because they did not believe it wise to set dates when the Bible tells us not to do so.[2] Some Adventists repudiated their date setting, swallowed their pride, and returned to their former churches. William Miller himself did

---

[1] Ellen G. White, *Spiritual Gifts*, Vol. 1, pp 139-140.

[2] Ibid. p. 139

this. Some continued to set dates for the return of Christ. The Adventists who would later become Seventh-day Adventists, initiated by an idea/vision that occurred to Hiram Edson, changed their focus from the earth being cleansed by the coming of the Lord to the heavenly sanctuary. They began to teach that all the events that took place on October 22, 1844, took place in Heaven. There, they believed, Jesus started for the first time his Day of Atonement ministry in heaven. It was then that He went into the Most Holy Place for the first time. This meant that the judgment had begun on that date and not before. This led the early Adventists to study the Old Testament sanctuary in great detail. They believed this held the key to their identity as a people.[3]

One reason the doctrine of the *sanctuary*, (another way of saying the investigative judgment in Adventist circles) is so important to Adventists (many ministers and other denominational workers have lost their positions because of their scriptural concerns in relation to this teaching) is that *the very identity* of the church as the "one true remnant church" hinges on this point. The focus on the Old Covenant sanctuary furniture caused them to look at the Ark of the Covenant containing the Ten Commandments. This, in turn, became a central focus for them. It caused them to place great emphasis on the keeping of the Law.[4] The sacredness of the seventh-day Sabbath came from the *sanctuary* (investigative judgment) focus. The doctrine of soul sleep was developed from this as well. Adventists realized that the investigative judgment would have no significance if the saints from the past were already in heaven and the lost were already in hell. If this were the case, an investigative judgment would have no significance.

---

[3] Dale Ratzlaff, *The Cultic Doctrine of Seventh-day Adventists*, (Glendale AZ, Life Assurance Ministries, 1996) For further study on the history and doctrinal development of the Adventist church read this careful analysis of the centerpiece of SDA theology and worldview.

[4] Ellen G. White, Early Writings, p 33.

In order to hold on to their Adventist worldview, the Adventists focused on the texts of Scripture that refer to death as sleep. They realized that any other view would undermine the investigative judgment. They therefore made this doctrine a test of fellowship. To question this teaching would mean questioning the sanctuary and the Adventist identity. Ellen White had been so forceful about the importance of the sanctuary doctrine that to question it would be to question *her authority*. Since the "Spirit of Prophecy" and the Sabbath are identifying marks of God's "one and only true remnant church," questioning the *sanctuary doctrine* became tantamount to rejecting the very heart of the church's identity.

We will not go into great detail in examining this doctrine because the Sabbath is the first and primary SDA doctrine that most people will encounter and is usually the drawing card Adventists use to attract new converts. Those claims will be the focus of the remainder of this book. However, I will include this brief summary of the problems with the investigative judgment doctrine because of its centrality to the church identity that few from the outside will ever fully realize.

The following questions that Adventists must answer in order for the doctrine to be scripturally viable came from Ex-Seventh-day Adventist minister Phillip Wilson and were recently printed by Sidney Cleveland.

1. It should be explained why the context of Daniel 8 is not considered and why the question of Daniel 8:13 is ignored, when seeking to interpret its answer given in Daniel 8:14
2. It must be proved the 2300 evening and morning sacrifices equal 2300 full days, when there is no conclusive evidence from Daniel 8:14 itself (and no other test of Scripture to confirm) that it means full days.

3. It must not only be proved that a day equals a year in prophecy but that an evening and a morning sacrifice equal one year.
4. In the face of contextual implication that the 2300-year period would commence when the daily sacrifice was suspended, it must be argued that it began, rather, in 457 B.C.—a date which had nothing to do with taking away the regular burnt offering.
5. It must be proved that the heavenly sanctuary is meant, when the context refers to the earthly sanctuary and activity against it by the little horn.
6. It must be proved that the cleansing of the sanctuary means cleansing it from the confessed sins of the saints, when the context refers to cleansing it from pollution by the desolating activities of the little horn.
7. It must be proved that confessed sins defile the sanctuary, and that the blood of individual sin offerings was taken into the sanctuary, that such blood was sin laden, and, therefore, defiled the holy places.
8. It must be assumed that 490 years are cut off from the 2300 years, when there is nothing in Daniel 8 or 9 that requires it.
9. It must be assumed that the 2300 years and the 490 years begin together, although there is no proof of this.
10. It must be maintained that the reconsecration of the sanctuary in Daniel 8:14, as well as the anointing of the sanctuary in Daniel 9:24 are not the same, but are separated by nearly 2000 years.
11. It must be proved that there is both contextual and linguistic linkage between Daniel 8:14 and Leviticus 16.

12. It must be demonstrated that the word *issued* in Daniel 9:25 refers to the kingly decree and that Artaxerxes made such a decree to restore and rebuild Jerusalem, when there is no evidence that he did.
13. It must be proved that the cleansing of the sanctuary commenced not just in 1844, but on October 22, 1844. Since such detail is not in the Bible, it must be shown that Karaites did celebrate the Day of Atonement on October 22, 1844, and that their calendar is more reliable than the orthodox rabbinical calendar. This entire exercise depends, of course, upon proving the cleansing of the sanctuary in Daniel 8:14 is the same as that typified in Leviticus 16.
14. It must be explained why, in giving the 2300 days a New Testament application, it is necessary to incorporate the Jewish Day of Atonement since SDAs teach that after the Cross, Judaism as a system was disqualified; the practices of the annual holy days ceased; and that the church is now the true Israel of God.
15. It must be shown that the antitypical day of atonement began in 1844, and it must be explained why Christ's great act of atonement (at Calvary) is not the day of atonement, but is separated from it by 1800 years.
16. It must be proved that the two-apartment schema of the Old Testament sanctuary parallels a two-apartment ministry by Christ in the heavenly sanctuary, when Hebrews does not suggest such a conclusion.
17. It must be shown that there are two apartments in the heavenly sanctuary, and that Christ moved from the holy place to the most holy in 1844. It must be explained also how, when the New

Testament says that Christ entered God's presence and sat down on the throne in the heavenly sanctuary (as Hebrews 9:12 says), this only means the first apartment in heaven.

18. It must be shown further why Christ must function as a priest after the order of Aaron, when Hebrews teaches that He has transcended that priesthood and functions as a priest after the order of Melchizedek.
19. It must be proved that the judgment that began in 1844 was an investigative judgment only for the professed people of God—not a judgment of the wicked horn or of Babylon.
20. It must be shown this [judgment] is what Revelation 14:7 is describing, though it gives no such details on this trial of the saints. Does Revelation 14:7 refer to this investigative judgment? Or does it refer to the great judgment hour of God that commenced at the Cross?[5]

One final note: the book of Hebrews does not indicate anything like an investigative judgment. In that book, the new ministry of Christ in heaven is contrasted with the old ministry of the Aaronic priesthood. Notice what is written in Hebrews:

> Therefore it was necessary that the copies of the things in the heavens should be purified with these, but the heavenly things themselves with *better sacrifices* than these. For Christ has not entered the holy places made with hands, which are copies of the true, but into heaven itself, now to appear in the presence of God for us; not that He should offer Himself often, as the high priest

[5] Sydney Cleveland, *White Washed*, (Glendale Arizona, Life Assurance Ministries, 2000) p. 154-156.

> enters the Most Holy Place every year with blood of another—He then would have had to suffer often since the foundation of the world; but *now, once at the end of the ages*, He has appeared to put away sin by the sacrifice of Himself. And as it is appointed for men to die once, but after this the judgment, so Christ was offered once to bear the sins of many. To those who eagerly wait for Him He will appear a second time, apart from sin, for salvation. Heb. 9:23-28

Hebrews makes it so plain that Jesus' work of atonement was completed at the Cross. He went straight to the Father's side to minister there for us. The Day of Atonement imagery had been fulfilled, the penalty paid. When our lives come to an end we will face the judgment based on whether or not we received the gift of grace. There is no gap implied here. No waiting for 1844 to roll around. No, the Day of Atonement was the Cross! The old system was just a shadow, not the reality itself. Jesus was a better sacrifice!

For us, the sanctuary doctrine was weak at best. The scriptural evidence was in no way compelling unless there was a vested interest in making it work. Even then, honest scholarship must admit the weakness of the position. In light of the problems with the authority of Ellen White and the issues associated with the investigative judgment, we launched into our study of the Sabbath. Even though we had to face fears that had been ingrained into us by the teachings of the church and specifically by Ellen White's writings, the challenge of the Scriptures to test or prove all these things required careful study to see if these things are true or not. So with the very real threat of losing our livelihood, the respect of the community we had served for many years, family relationships and friendships, we started to study the authenticity of the seventh-day Sabbath.

CHAPTER SEVEN

THE SABBATH IN COLOSSIANS

It was important that Paula and I each take separate journeys with our study. We each had unique issues that were of concern to us. Therefore, we tried to do our own study and not influence one another concerning the outcome. I will take you with me and share with you the presuppositions I used as a basis for my study.

First, I believe that all of the Bible is God's Word and is inspired by Him. I assume full inspiration of the Scriptures. The second foundational presupposition dealt with application of that inspiration. I do not believe that every portion of Scripture has equal authority on a given subject. Certain portions of the Scriptures have greater authority than others. For example, a passage that was specifically written to address a particular theme will have greater value in a discussion than one that mentions it incidentally. Greater authority must be given to Scriptures that were originally intended to teach on a specific topic.

Finally, as it relates to Christian behavior and instruction, the New Testament interprets the Old, not the other way around. They are both inspired, but there needs to be greater emphasis on the New Testament by the very nature of what is meant by the word Testament.

The word Testament or Covenant means the same thing as a *will,* or some other legal contract. My wife and I have made out several wills during our marriage. We had a will before we had kids. We had a will made after the birth of our first child. We made another after the second child, and recently we updated our will again. Now if we were to die in some tragedy, which will would be binding for our executor to follow? The most recent, or newest one, of course. The previous legal contract becomes null and void once the new one takes effect. That is why only the *last* will and testament is read and followed. There may be some carry over from one will to another, but such carry over will always be stipulated in the new will. What does not carry over will not be specified in the new contract. The same thing would be true of financial contracts. We just finished refinancing our house. Our new agreement is for a lesser interest rate and with another financing company. The purpose is the same. It allows us to make payments we can afford for a period of time in order to eventually own the house. Much of the language in the new contract is the same. Many of the details are similar. But much is changed as well. Primarily, the difference is in the interest rate, the fixed rate versus a floating rate. But there are other details that differ as well. We do not send the check to the same company any more. Our obligations to the old organization have been satisfied by the new contract. We keep our old contract around for tax purposes, but it is no longer binding. That loan has been paid off by the new lending institution. Therefore we are free from the old contract and bound to the new.

The same thing is true of the Old and New Covenants. There are wonderful truths about God found in the Old Covenant. However, it is imperative that we remember that the New *Covenant* or *Testament* is the one that is binding. There is much history and background information that helps us understand God better. But to go first to the Old Testament for application of God's will for our lives would be to get things out of order. The New Testament was written to give us a more full revelation of God's workings in human history. It gives us the fullest revelation of all, Jesus Christ. Since we must apply the message of Jesus to our personal lives as post-Cross Christians, the Epistles were written specifically for that purpose. Jesus came to fulfill much of the system of Judaism, for example. He came to fulfill some of the aspects of the Old Covenant or Testament. How do we know which ones? The Gospels do not spell out which ones. The Epistles do that. So it is of crucial importance that we remember the application principles when studying the Scriptures.

I went first to the New Testament (covenant or will) and specifically to the Epistles to see what is taught there about the application of the Sabbath to Christians today. Then I went to Jesus' life to see if He made room for such an interpretation in His life and ministry. I asked myself if Jesus' life and ministry prepared the way for what I had learned in the Epistles. Finally, I went back to the Old Testament to see if what is written there agrees with the Epistles and Jesus on the subject. In this way, I made every effort to focus on the application sections of the Scriptures first.

The first text I studied is found in Colossians two. (I am using the New King James version of the Bible unless otherwise indicated, and all of the emphases are my own.) In the book of Colossians, Paul is addressing a syncretistic heresy that is a mixture of angel worship and ascetic practices. But mixed into it all is the Judaizing element (Jewish legalistic Christians who were requiring Jewish law of the Gentile believers) that is trying to influence these new Christians. In the Colossians two passage, the focus is on the Jewish part of the heresy. Starting with verse 11, Paul focuses on the fact that circumcision has been replaced by baptism; therefore circumcision is no longer required. Then he points out that the record of our sins is nailed to the Cross as soon as we accept Jesus. Finally, Paul discusses the last two Jewish distinctives. Notice the following verses:

> So let no one judge you in food or in drink, or regarding a festival or a new moon or sabbaths, which are a shadow of things to come, but the substance is of Christ. Col. 2:16-17.

It is crystal clear in these verses that Paul is specifically addressing the New Covenant interpretation of the Old Covenant Jewish laws. No other religion emphasized circumcision, food laws, and sabbaths. There can be no confusion as to what Paul is addressing here. Paul is telling the Colossians not to let these people, who were trying to push their Jewish religious views and customs on the Gentile believers, lay a guilt trip on them about the *food laws, the festivals, new moons, or the sabbaths,* because these were part of the system that prefigured, or pointed forward to Christ. They were a "shadow of things to come."

During my entire life in the Adventist Church I was taught that the Sabbath is an eternal institution, and it will be forever. It is morally binding on all people for all time. I had also learned in my studies in the SDA institutions that the sabbaths mentioned here (Col. 2:16-17) could not be the weekly seventh-day Sabbath, but rather these sabbaths referred to the ceremonial sabbaths, such as the Passover, Pentecost or Tabernacles. This passage was focused on these ceremonial sabbaths of the Jewish feasts, and not the weekly Sabbath. Later, however, I was most amazed to discover that this is definitely *not* the case. Throughout the Old Testament, this same construction is used. Paul was simply reiterating a formula that was used repeatedly to refer to the entire old system, including the seventh-day Sabbath. This same construction is found in ascending or descending order repeatedly throughout the Old Testament. There can be no mistake what he meant. The "sabbaths" in this common Old

Testament construction always refer to the weekly Sabbath. To try to make this Colossians passage refer to ceremonial festival sabbaths ignores this construction.

First of all, Leviticus 23 lists all of the religious feasts. At the top of the list is the seventh-day Sabbath followed by the other feasts. The seventh-day Sabbath is listed right alongside all of the other sabbaths. In passages throughout the Old Testament, the same order is found in either ascending or descending order, clearly including the weekly Sabbath with the special feasts. Notice the following verses:

> . . . to stand every morning to thank and praise the LORD, and likewise at evening; and at every presentation of a burnt offering to the LORD on *the Sabbaths and on the New Moons and on the set feasts*, by number according to the ordinance governing them, regularly before the LORD. 1 Chron. 23:30-31

> Behold, I am building a temple for the name of the LORD my God, to dedicate it to Him, to burn before Him sweet incense, for the continual showbread, for the burnt offerings morning and evening, on the *Sabbaths, on the New Moons, and on the set feasts* of the LORD our God. 2 Chron. 2:4

> Also we made ordinances for ourselves, to exact from ourselves yearly one-third of a shekel for the service of the house of our God: for the showbread, for the regular grain offering, for the regular burnt offering of the *Sabbaths, the New Moons, and the set feasts.* Neh. 10:32-33

> I will also cause all her mirth to cease, *her feast days, her New Moons, her Sabbaths*—all her appointed feasts. And I will destroy her vines and her fig trees, of which she has said, 'These are my wages that my lovers have

> given me.' so I will make them a forest, and the beasts of the field shall eat them. Hosea 2:11, 12

> Then it shall be the prince's part to give burnt offerings, grain offerings, and drink offerings, *at the feasts, the New Moons, the Sabbaths*, and at all the appointed seasons of the house of Israel. He shall prepare the sin offering, the grain offering, the burnt offering, and the peace offerings to make atonement for the house of Israel. Ezek. 45:17

Notice the construction. The order of Sabbaths, the new moons, and the festivals is clear and distinct. There can be no mistaking that this refers to the weekly, the monthly and the seasonal festivals. Throughout the Old Testament, the same construction is used. The weekly, the monthly, the seasonal, and sometimes the yearly or sabbatical years are included. Sometimes the order is reversed, but the same principle applies.

The "sabbaths" referred to in Colossians 2:16-17 are therefore referring to the seventh-day Sabbaths. It would be redundant and totally out of literary character for this to refer to the appointed feasts. To make it do so would make the passage read "Let no one judge you regarding festivals, new moons, or festivals." That would not make sense. Even Samuele Bacchiocchi (noted sabbatarian author) admits that this is the case. He agrees that the weekly Sabbath is what is being referred to here.[1] He does go on to say that it is not the proper keeping of the Sabbath that is being discussed, but the perversion of the keeping of the day that is the focus.

The biblical problem with Bacchiocchi's theory is that the text continues by describing these sabbaths and festivals as "shadows of things to come," the "reality is Christ." These

---

[1]Samuele Bacchiocchi, *Sabbath Under Crossfire* (Biblical Perspectives, 1998) p. 245-248.

religious holidays, including the Sabbath, were symbols pointing forward to Jesus. They were typological prefigurations of Jesus.[2] How could the perversion of a symbol be a shadow or prefiguration of Christ? How could a perversion prefigure? That doesn't make any sense. The most reasonable rendering of the text is that the weekly Sabbath is included in the ceremonial/sacrificial system that was *fulfilled in Christ*! No other explanation makes sense. No other interpretation does justice to the New Testament context or the Old Testament construction.

When I first read this the way Paul clearly intended it, I could not believe what I was reading! Paul was making a radical transitional statement here! The Sabbath fulfilled in Christ! Could it be true? Could it be that the rest of the Sabbath was a symbol of a greater rest in the person of Jesus Christ? More questions came to mind. What about the Ten Commandments? Aren't they eternal? What about the Sabbath being from Creation? I had so many questions. I had to search them out. The hunger to understand and learn was overpowering the fear that had been placed in me since childhood.

---

[2]Ibid. 246-248.

CHAPTER EIGHT

THE SABBATH IN GALATIANS

The next stop was the book of Galatians where Paul again makes reference to the Sabbath in his scathing rebuke of the Judaizing heresy that had threatened the Galatian church. Here Paul explains the purpose of the Law to these Gentile believers. To get the feel of the argument he is using, we must start back in Galatians.

> Now to Abraham and his Seed were the promises made. He does not say "And to seeds," as of many, but as of one, "And to your seed," who is Christ. And this I say, that the law, which was four hundred and thirty years later, cannot annul the covenant that was confirmed before by God in Christ, that it should make the promises of no effect." Gal. 3:16, 17.

What Paul is saying is that the covenant with Abraham was given pre-Law. And it was made with Christ in mind. Let's continue with verse 18.

> For if the inheritance is of the law, it is no longer of promise; but God gave it to Abraham by promise. What purpose then does the law serve? It was *added* because

> of transgressions '*till* the Seed should come to whom the promise was made: Gal. 3:18, 19.

Paul is saying that the Law was added well after the promises to Abraham, until Christ. There was a definite *beginning* and *ending* of the Law. This is crucial to understand in order to follow Paul's argument. Now notice verses 23 and following:

> But before faith came, we were kept under guard by the law, kept for the faith which would afterward to be revealed. Therefore the law was our tutor to bring us to Christ, that we might be justified by faith. But after faith has come, *we are no longer under a tutor*. Gal. 3:23-25

Paul continues with his discussion, ending Galatians 3 with the famous statement in verse 29.

> And if you are Christ's, then you are Abraham's seed, and heirs according to the promise. Gal. 3:29.

What Paul is saying here is that the promise of Christ came *before* the Law. It is independent of the Law. The Law was *added* to show us our need of Christ. It was our tutor to bring us to Christ that we might be justified by *faith*. Clearly Paul is pointing out that the Law was a *temporary* institution to show us our need of Christ. But when we accept Jesus, we are under the covenant, which was pre-circumcision and pre-Law, the covenant with Abraham. The Christian now stands with righteous Abraham, an heir of the promise, bypassing the entire Law era! I had never seen the significance of this passage before! I had to read and re-read it. I encourage you to sit down with the book of Galatians to read and digest it for yourself. The message is so powerful and liberating! It also sets the stage for understanding the rest of the book.

In Galatians 4 Paul continues his argument by discussing the absurdity of going back to the "elementary principles," or "weak and beggarly elements" which contextually are a clear reference to going back to Law-based living. Continuing on, we read,

> But now after you have known God, or rather are known by God, how is it that you turn again to the weak and beggarly elements, to which you desire again to be in bondage. *You observe days and months and seasons and years.* I am afraid for you, lest I have labored for you in vain. Gal. 4:9-11.

I could hardly believe my eyes as I read these verses. I had read it many times before, but never understood it. This time the words seemed to jump off the page at me, much like the "Magic Eye" hidden pictures I mentioned earlier. Could Paul have been any clearer? Knowing the pattern for religious holidays in the Old Testament, it suddenly clarified for me what was at issue here. The Judaizers had been teaching these new Christians that they should keep the Sabbaths and the rest of the feasts as part of their commitment to Christ. The days, months, seasons, and years follow the same pattern of the Jewish holiday system, including the seventh-day Sabbath. The Judaizers were telling the Galatians that they *must* keep the Sabbath and the other feasts. *But* Paul is clearly saying that observing these holidays is *not required* of Gentile Christians. He sees that doing so could be *dangerous* to their maturity as Christians. He is saying that these things do *not* have value because the Law was a temporary institution. Christians are accepted on the basis of Jesus' fulfillment of the Law and treated as pre-Law Abrahamic descendants! The message of Galatians seemed to literally come to life for me. Those hard to understand passages suddenly made perfect sense!

I must take a moment to dwell on the importance of the book of Galatians. The book was written for the purpose of making a clear delineation between what was to be classified as Old Covenant and what was to be included in the New. The book of Galatians has one basic theme from beginning to end, and that is to clarify what the Gospel really is. Paul clearly defines for these new Christians what is genuine good news and what is a perversion. To make his point absolutely clear, he states his own credentials in no uncertain terms. In Galatians 1:1 he declares his *apostleship*, the highest office in the church. He is careful to remind his readers that he was not appointed by men but by Jesus Christ himself. Secondly, he states that he got his message directly *by revelation* from Jesus Himself. There were no other humans involved in the delivery of the message. Thirdly, in Galatians 2:6-10 he reminds the Galatians that *the apostles* in Jerusalem put their stamp of approval on the soundness of his doctrinal position. And finally, He had the *authority* to take the Apostle Peter to task when he succumbed to pressure from the Jewish Christians. Paul publicly rebuked the influential apostle for withdrawing from the Gentiles in table fellowship. Paul's message is therefore absolutely above question or debate. He is writing this Epistle to settle once and for all the issue of what constitutes the true and authentic Gospel. *This places the letter to the Galatians first and foremost in authority in issues of Law versus Grace.* Paul even states in Galatians 1:8-9 that if an angel from heaven tells you something else, let him be eternally condemned. *Angelic messages must be tested by this Epistle! One cannot just believe any angel!*

Now let us focus on what was revealed to him about the Law. Paul points out that it was a *temporary* institution that was "*added*" 430 years after Abraham and was in effect "*until*" the Christ would come. He is absolutely clear that circumcision, the food laws,[1] and the Sabbath laws were specifically included in that which was no longer in effect. He uses the same construction found in Colossians 2, making it crystal clear that the seventh-day Sabbath was also temporary.

At this point I realized that the issue of the Old Covenant food laws was intertwined with the Sabbath regulations. I will not take significant time to discuss this in this book. I will, however, mention a few scriptural references that are important to notice in this regard. First of all, the Gospel of Mark records the discussion of Jesus and the Pharisees over the issue of eating with unwashed hands. The discussion moves on to what truly matters as far as what *clean* and *unclean* meant to Jesus. In Mark 7 we read:

> Again Jesus called the crowd to him and said, "Listen to me, everyone, and understand this. Nothing outside a man can make him '*unclean*' by going into him. Rather, it is what comes out of a man that makes him '*unclean*.' After he had left the crowd and entered the house, his disciples asked him about this parable. "Are you so dull?" he asked. "Don't you see that nothing that enters a man from the outside can make him '*unclean*?' For it doesn't go into his heart but into his stomach, and then out of his body." (*In saying this, Jesus declared all foods clean.*) He went on: 'What comes out of a man is what makes him '*unclean*.' For from within, out of men's hearts, come evil thoughts, sexual immorality, theft, murder, adultery, greed, malice, deceit, lewdness,

[1] This issue of table fellowship with gentiles was the result of what the Old Covenant law said about certain foods. The Levitical code (Leviticus 11) forbids the use of "unclean foods." For a Jew to eat with a person who ate such forbidden foods was to become unclean himself. Some of the Jewish Christians believed that these laws were still binding, and Peter was influenced by them to withdraw from the Gentiles to avoid criticism.

> envy, slander, arrogance and folly. All these evils come from inside and make a man '*unclean*.' Mark 7:14-23 (NIV).

Mark's comment here was written many years later from the perspective of the New Covenant understanding of the apostles. He clearly understood Jesus to be making an end to the food laws.

Acts 10-11 records the story of Peter and the vision of the unclean animals that he was told to kill and eat. The primary application of this vision was to make it clear to Peter that he was to call no man common or unclean any more. But behind the vision is another truth. What was it that made the Gentiles unclean? It was what they ate. It was the food laws behind the scenes that made the Gentiles unclean to the observant Jews. The point is once again made that the food laws were not considered binding by the apostles. In First Timothy 4 the Holy Spirit warns against heresies that teach abstinence from certain foods:

> Now the Spirit expressly says that in latter times some will depart from the faith, giving heed to *deceiving spirits* and doctrines of demons, speaking lies in hypocrisy, having their own conscience seared with a hot iron, forbidding to marry, and commanding to abstain from foods which God created to be received with thanksgiving by those who believe and know the truth. For *every creature of God is good, and nothing is to be refused if it is received with thanksgiving*; for it is sanctified by the word of God and prayer. 1 Tim 4:1-5.

Here a warning is attached to making an issue of food laws. These were understood by the apostles to be dividing issues between believers that must not be tolerated.[2] Paul warns that one of the last day deceptions will be the re-introduction of the food laws as a requirement for Christians. He declares that such teachings are the doctrines of demons. Those are hard words, but must be noted because of the seriousness of the warning.[3] The Epistle to the Galatians and the Epistle to the Colossians are in perfect agreement with the rest of the New Testament on this issue.

There is much instruction in Galatians about moral living. While the Sabbath laws and food laws are not binding, it must *not* be seen as an indication that Paul is condoning immorality. He is actually calling the true Christian to a higher morality, the morality of the Spirit. He appeals to the Spirit and not to the Law. He points to Christ, not the Law, as a point of reference. The appeal is never to the Law in Galatians, or in any of Paul's writings for that matter. He includes the Sabbath with those things that are no longer binding, and possibly dangerous, if made a requirement for salvation. Paul clearly teaches responsible morality and I will go into that later, but his appeal is to Christ living in you, not to Law.

> I say then: Walk in the Spirit, and you shall not fulfill the lust of the flesh. For the flesh lusts against the Spirit and the Spirit against the flesh; and these are contrary to

---

[2] This is another example of Adventists ignoring the New Covenant Scriptures in favor of the Old. Interestingly, even in the Old Testament, the Gentiles were never asked to abide by these clean/unclean laws. Notice the command to Noah upon his exit from the ark in Genesis 9:3. It made all living creatures good for food. The specific laws to Israel were temporary and for the people of Israel only.

[3] Many people in the SDA church are not aware that Ellen G. White for a time forbade marriage. While she did not tell people that they could not have a mate, she did forbid marriage relations for those that were missionaries because the resulting children would be a hindrance to the work. This was a cause of guilt and frustration among the missionaries. The details are found in Document DF 97c in the White Estate vault.

one another, so that you do not do the things that you wish. But if you are led by the Spirit, you are not under the Law. Now the works of the flesh are evident, which are: adultery, fornication, uncleanness, lewdness, idolatry, sorcery, hatred, contentions, jealousies, outbursts of wrath, selfish ambitions, dissensions, heresies, envy, murders, drunkenness, revelries, and the like; of which I tell you beforehand, just as I also told you in time past, that those who practice such things will not inherit the kingdom of God. But the fruit of the Spirit is love, joy, peace, longsuffering, kindness, goodness, faithfulness, gentleness, self-control. Against such there is no law. Gal 5:16-23.

CHAPTER NINE

THE SABBATH IN THE OTHER EPISTLES

The next text I studied was Romans 14. Here Paul takes a softer approach. The Jewish and Gentile Christians are living side by side. There are some who are highly concerned about food that might have been offered to idols, and others are saying that idols do not exist, so they eat just about anything. But some are judging one another's spirituality based on these behaviors. Paul steps in to mediate in the dispute. It is in this context that the holiness of certain days over others comes up again. Here it is an issue of Christian unity, not one of requirement for salvation, so his approach is much more gentle. Notice how Romans 14 reads:

> One person esteems one day above another; another esteems every day alike. Let each be fully convinced in his own mind. He who observes the day, observes it to the Lord; and he who does not observe the day, to the Lord he does not observe it. Rom. 14:5-6.

Paul is again making the same basic statement, though in much gentler language. He is declaring once again, that the sacredness of days is no longer an issue for Christians.

As long as people are fully convinced in their own minds, he has no issue with people observing days as a part of their own spiritual discipline, but it must not become an issue of passing judgment on others. We find as we have seen before, *Sabbath should never be confused with a person's salvation.* Again, Paul makes Sabbath a non-issue for New Testament Christians. His instructions carry some strong implications for those who would make the Sabbath a "saving truth" or a standard by which to judge the orthodoxy of other Christians. I had to take a hard look at some of the things I had been taught and had myself taught while in the Adventist ministry. Under the teachings of the Adventist denomination I had been unconsciously ignoring these warnings and the truth of the New Covenant.

Next in my study, I went to the book of Hebrews, starting with Chapters 3 and 4. (It would be helpful to read this entire scripture before reading my comments.) As I began to study these chapters, I noticed that the word *today* is used 5 times. The emphasis in this passage is on an action that can and must take place today. I also noticed that the children of Israel did not enter God's rest because of unbelief. They rested on the Sabbath each week in the wilderness because if they hadn't they would have been executed for Sabbath breaking. Sabbath rest was not an option in those days; it was a life or death requirement. Even so, with the strict Sabbath observance of the Old Covenant, they did not enter into God's rest. Why? They missed out because of unbelief. Even when Joshua led them into the Promised Land, they still did not enter that rest. Now notice Hebrews 4:

> For we who have *believed* do enter that rest, . . . Since therefore it remains that some must enter it, and those to whom it was first preached did not enter because of disobedience, again He designates a certain day saying in David, "*Today,*" after such a long time as it has been said: "*Today*, if you will hear His voice, Do not harden

> your hearts." For if Joshua had given them rest, then he would not afterward have spoken of another day. There remains therefore a rest [*Sabbatismos* in Greek which means Sabbath-like rest] for the people of God. For he who has entered His rest has himself also ceased from his works as God did from His." Heb. 4:3-10

The author of Hebrews is saying that those who believe in Jesus are resting in a Sabbath-like rest. The key to rest is belief. The time to enter that rest is another day called *today*! It bears repeating that starting in Hebrews three, where this topic begins, the word *today* is mentioned five times.

The Sabbath-like *rest* that is offered to us in Christ is a *today* experience. It is ours today and every day as we trust in Christ's righteousness and rest from any trust in our own works. This is not an instruction to keep Sabbath, as I had been taught in the SDA schools. It is a daily rest experience in Jesus as we *rest* from our own works as He did from His. The day to enter that rest is today.

Here again I discovered that the New Testament considers the Sabbath to be a *fulfilled* institution. Here again the Scriptures clearly indicate that Jesus is our Sabbath-like rest. When we trust Him by faith, we are experiencing Sabbath-like rest each and every day of our lives! What a beautiful concept! Jesus is your Sabbath and mine when we trust daily in Him. My eyes were starting to see another perspective I had never seen before.

There are some who have tried to make this text a reason for continued Sabbath keeping, but that ignores the context of the passage. It also ignores the greater context of the book of Hebrews. The entire book is dedicated to showing the superiority of Christ over the Old Testament system. For example, Hebrews one emphasizes His superiority over the whole Old Testament Scriptures (Heb. 1:1-3). In verses four and following, He is shown as being superior to all the angels. In chapter three He is seen as being superior to Moses; in chapters 5-7 He is superior to all the priests, introducing a new order, the order of Melchizedek. In chapters 8-10 He is a greater sanctuary/temple, a greater sacrifice, and a greater covenant. The entire book of Hebrews is about Jesus being "superior to" and the "fulfillment of" the entire Old Testament/Covenant system. To try to say in the middle of this theme that Sabbath is a binding day for Christians, is to miss not only the context of Hebrews 3-4, but the larger context of the entire book. The logical point that the author is making is that *Jesus is a better Sabbath* than the old literal one-day-a-week rest. *He is our rest today and every day as we put our trust in him!* He is the true temple, the true Passover, the true Law, the *true Sabbath*! As I studied this out, my heart just burned within me as I saw the significance of Jesus in this book.

The next few passages in Hebrews underscore what the study had taught me thus far, but they made even clearer what the New Testament, or *new will*, teaches about what carries over from the Old. Notice the following selected verses from Hebrews 8-10. Please do not take my word. Refer to your own Bible and study for yourself. Study the context and the verses in between my selections to see if these things are so. Start with Chapter 8, right after the phrase in verse five that refers to the temple system as a "shadow of heavenly things." (There is an interesting similarity to Colossians. 2:16-17). Starting with verse six we read,

> But now, He has obtained a more excellent ministry inasmuch as He is also Mediator of a *better covenant*, which was established on better promises. For if that first covenant had been faultless, then no place would have been sought for a second. Heb. 8:6-7

> In that He says, "a New Covenant," He has made the first *obsolete*. Now what is becoming obsolete and growing old is ready to vanish away. Heb. 8:13

> And for this reason He is the Mediator of the New Covenant, by means of death, for the redemption of the transgressions under the first covenant, that those who are called may receive the promise of eternal inheritance. Heb. 9:15

> For the law, having a shadow of the good things to come, and not the very image of the things, can never with these same sacrifices, which they offer continually year by year, make those who approach perfect. Heb. 10:1

> . . . He takes away the first that He may establish the second. Heb. 10:9

The more I read the book of Hebrews, the more I started to see the "Magic Eye" picture I had missed before. Suddenly passages that I had never understood before became clear to me. I was seeing through *new glasses*. I had always studied the Scriptures with Old Covenant glasses on. Now that I was reading it with New Covenant glasses, I was seeing a whole new picture. I began to feel embarrassed that I had never seen it before. It was as if a *veil* had fallen from my eyes. I discovered at my next stop that this is precisely what had happened. Notice II Corinthians 3 with me, starting with the last phrase of verse five.

> . . .our sufficiency is from God, who also made us sufficient as ministers of the new covenant, not of the letter, but of the Spirit; for the letter kills but the Spirit gives life. But if the ministry of death, written and

> *engraved on stones,* was glorious, so that the children of Israel could not look steadily at the face of Moses because of the glory of his countenance, which glory was *passing away.* II Cor. 3:5-7

Now look at verses 13-18:

> . . .unlike Moses, who put a veil over his face so that the children of Israel could not look steadily at the end of what was passing away. But their minds were blinded. For until this day the same veil remains unlifted in the reading of the Old Testament, because the veil is taken away in Christ. But even to this day, when Moses is read, *a veil lies on their heart.* Nevertheless *when one turns to the Lord, the veil is taken away.* Now the Lord is the Spirit; and where the Spirit of the Lord is, there is liberty. But we all, with unveiled face, beholding as in a mirror the glory of the Lord, are being transformed into the same image from glory to glory, just as by the Spirit of the Lord. II Cor. 3:13-18

Paul declares that as long as our focus is on the Old Covenant, engraved on stones, it is as if we see things through a veil. But once we come to Christ fully, we start looking to Him instead of the Law. We lose the veil and our lives are transformed by looking to Jesus instead of the Law. As I studied these passages, I became convinced that a radical change had taken place in the Cross event, much greater than I had ever grasped before.

Next I visited the book of Ephesians. Here the Sabbath is not specifically mentioned, but the same message came through loud and clear.

> Therefore remember that you, once Gentiles in the flesh—who are called Uncircumcision by what is called the Circumcision made in the flesh by

> hands—that at that time you were without Christ, being aliens from the commonwealth of Israel and strangers from the covenants of promise, having no hope and without God in the world. But now in Christ Jesus you who once were far off have been brought near by the blood of Christ. For He Himself is our peace, who has made both one, and has broken down the middle wall of separation, *having abolished in His flesh the enmity, that is, the law of commandments contained in ordinances, so as to create in Himself one new man from the two, thus making peace, and that He might reconcile them both to God in one body through the Cross*, thereby putting to death the enmity. And He came and preached peace to you who were afar off and to those who were near. For through Him we both have access by one Spirit to the Father. Now, therefore, you are no longer strangers and foreigners, but fellow citizens with the saints and members of the household of God. Eph 2:11-19

As I read this passage I had to ask myself what were the commandments and ordinances that once separated the Jews the Gentiles? This could refer to only three things, the same three things we have been studying about all along, namely, circumcision, the food laws and Sabbath observance. My eyes were opening to see that the dividing wall of hostility that Christ broke down really did include all of the Law, including the specific laws that divided Jews and Gentiles. The Sabbath, the feasts, the clean and uncleanness laws, the sacrificial system, and circumcision, were all fulfilled in Jesus. Thereby Christ has truly made all believers one in Himself.

CHAPTER TEN

The Sabbath in Acts

Another passage I looked at was Acts 15. In this passage we find the leaders of the church gathered in Jerusalem to decide what laws would be binding on the Gentile Christians. There were those, the Judaizers, who were teaching that unless a person is "circumcised according to the Law of Moses they could not be saved" (15:1) These Judaizers, a sect of the Pharisees who had become Christian, were putting the requirements of circumcision and keeping the Law of Moses on all new converts. They wanted all new converts to become "Circumcised and keep the Law of Moses." Paul and Barnabas were adamant that such requirements should not be placed on new believers. Peter agreed with them and said,

> Now therefore, why do you test God by putting a yoke on the neck of the disciples which neither our fathers nor we were able to bear? Acts 15:10.

He goes on in verse 11 to point out that we are saved by grace, not the Law.[1]

At this point it is necessary to highlight the fact that the entrance sign of becoming a Jew was the sign of circumcision. A male was not considered a full Son of Israel until he was circumcised. Once one was circumcised, he was then required to keep all of the laws. This included the Sabbath which was the continuing sign of allegiance to the Old Covenant[2] as we will soon see. Obviously the sign of circumcision was not clearly visible, but the continuing sign of the Sabbath was very obvious. Both men and women participated in this sign. Failure to keep Sabbath was punishable by death. (Ex. 31:14) The Sabbath sign, however, was not expected of those who were not orthodox Jews. The entrance sign of circumcision was a prerequisite sign for entrance into the Jewish community. Once one had become circumcised, he was then under obligation to keep the rest of the Law, including the Sabbath.

This can be understood today with baptism and church membership. Each church has a set of standards or core expectations that are part of that community of believers. Once one is baptized and makes the decision to become a member of that community, he/she is then expected to live in accordance with these core expectations. However, if one has not taken the prerequisite step and been baptized or has not chosen membership, there is no obligation to these values or standards. Circumcision was the entrance commitment for membership into the Jewish community.

---

[1] Notice the use of the word yoke attached to the Law. This is the same way Paul referenced the Law in Galatians 5:1 calling it a yoke of bondage. Interestingly, Jesus instructs His followers to take His yoke upon them because His yoke is easy and His burden is light. Jesus is a light yoke, the Law is a yoke of bondage. See Matthew 11:28-30.
[2] Dale Ratzlaff, *Sabbath in Crisis* (Glendale, AZ, 1990) pp 180-182 for expanded discussion.

Without circumcision there was no obligation to the rest of the law. This is why circumcision was the issue that was so hotly debated. Sabbath observance was not expected of the uncircumcised, non-Jewish community around them.

The rules regarding Sabbath involved not carrying a burden, not building a fire, not traveling, and of course, not working in any way on that day. This was to apply to the Jews and also to the stranger within their gates or their households. It was not applicable to the strangers who "sojourned among them." Only those within their gates were required to keep Sabbath. There were also the food laws and the laws of uncleanness that were part of this system and marked the Jews as separate from the rest of the world around them. It is clearly these requirements that Peter was referring to as a burden too heavy to bear.

In Acts 15 the church leaders came to a solution. They decided not to place on the new converts any of the specific regulations that were part of the covenantal system of Judaism. They did not require the entrance sign, so the rest of the laws would not apply either—just as today we do not require someone who is not baptized to follow all the guidelines of a particular church. The regulations that they did require had their origins in the Noahic covenant (see Gen. 6-10, which included worship of the true God, avoiding things strangled, blood, and sexual immorality). These were considered by Jews everywhere to be required of *all people* since the covenant with Noah applied to all humans. Leviticus 17-18 expands on these and defines what is meant by these regulations. In each case in Leviticus 17-18, it is made clear that they are binding on the "stranger that sojourns among you." (Notice the clear distinction between this group and the "stranger that is within your gates.") Notice also Acts 15:20 where these regulations *are* considered binding on the new converts. The reason being that there were Jewish people in every city who read the Law of Moses each Sabbath, and they would expect someone who fears the Lord, even if not a part of the Jewish circumcised Sabbath-keeping observant community, to follow these guidelines. Why? Because the Jews believed they were universal requirements based on the Noahic covenant. For any Jew to respect a Christian, the believer must be seen as at least following the Noahic laws. Hence, the early church council decided to require Noahic covenant stipulations on all Christians, but did not require the Mosaic regulations.[3] The ruling was repeated again in the letter that went out to the Gentile churches (Acts 15:28-29). The result was great rejoicing in the church. The Sabbath was *not* one of the requirements placed on these new believers.

Some have tried to make an argument for the validity of Sabbath observance from the comparative silence concerning Sabbath debates in the New Testament. They contend that since there was no big debate over the Sabbath in the early church and there was so much said about circumcision, that Sabbath must have still been required. If circumcision was such a big deal, wouldn't Sabbath have been a bigger issue? Not at all! Where there was no entrance to the Jewish community through circumcision, there was no Sabbath requirement. The entrance sign came first. The continuing sign was immaterial if the initial sign was not present. This is why the circumcision battle was fought so intensely. It was the starting point to all Law observance. Where there is no circumcision there is no Law. Sabbath would have no relevance without the entrance into the Jewish community.

Another argument is often used by sabbatarians. It states that we should follow Paul's custom. He attended the synagogue on the Sabbath and so should everyone else. It was Paul's custom to go to the synagogue on the Sabbath. But does this mean that he thought it was still binding? Not necessarily. The problem with the argument is that it fails to

---

[3] Notice also that the Noahic food laws allowed all creatures to be used for food (Gen. 9:3). Therefore, Acts 15 does not require the clean/unclean distinction that was part of the Sinai Covenant.

take into consideration Paul's *motivation* for being there. Was Paul going to the synagogue because he believed it was a binding obligation for Christians? No! It was Paul's custom to go to the synagogue to *evangelize* the Jews. He would go to the Jews first (Rom.1:16) whenever he went to a new city. He would teach in the synagogues in each city until he was thrown out, and then he would meet with Gentiles. His intention was to *reach out* to Jews, not because he was obligated to keep Sabbath.

CHAPTER ELEVEN

THE SABBATH IN REVELATION

Another passage that needed to be examined from my perspective as an Adventist was Revelation 12:17. This is the verse, along with other related passages in the Apocalypse I mentioned earlier, that has great eschatological significance for Seventh-day Adventists. It forms the basis for their identification of themselves as the one and only true church of the last days. The focus of their eschatological claims centers on Sabbath observance as the identifying mark of the "remnant" church.

In the ancient near eastern covenants, the sign or seal of a covenant or agreement was found in the segment of the document that identified the ruling party or suzerain, their position of authority, and their rights as such. It also stated what was expected of the subject party and what would be the outward sign of obedience or loyalty to the suzerain. The Old Covenant, like other ancient near eastern documents, followed this format, and the Sabbath was clearly this sign or seal of the Ten Commandments. It stated that God as Creator was the authority figure and the subjects were to remember this by keeping the Sabbath. Exodus 31:12-18 clearly states that the Sabbath was the sign of the

Covenant, to ignore this sign was seen as disloyalty to God and punishable by death.[1]

It is because of this Old Covenant Sabbath law that the Adventist Church declares that the "Seal of God" is still the seventh-day Sabbath in the New Covenant. No discontinuance of the Old Covenant is recognized. Their Old Covenant eyeglasses make this interpretation of Revelation particularly exclusive and behavioral in nature.

Furthermore, they take the 1260 day prophecies of Revelation 12-13 (the passage that refers to the *mark of the beast*) to be literal years and attribute these years to the time period of the authority of the Roman Catholic Church. They believe that the Catholic Church attempted to change the Sabbath to Sunday. This "beast power" (interpreted to be the Catholic Church) along with all Protestants that insist on Sunday worship, will one day force all people to observe Sunday instead of Sabbath.[2] They view this to be in direct rebellion against the Covenant sign or Seal of God, the Sabbath. The resulting false worship will become the mark of the beast, and only Sabbath keepers will receive the "Seal of God." Therefore, Adventists believe and teach in their *Revelation Seminars* and *Prophecy Crusades*, that Sabbath observance is the final test of loyalty to God for all mankind. They emphasize Revelation 12:17 as their identity test because it describes the remnant church as keeping the commandments of God (Sabbath observance) and having the testimony of Jesus (Ellen G. White's prophecies).

There are numerous problems with this conclusion. But we will just look at the two that truly opened my eyes as I studied with the New Covenant glasses on. First, the New Testament does *not* anywhere call the Sabbath the

---

[1] Ibid. p. 27-28.

[2] Ellen G. White, *The Great Controversy*, p. 605 See also *Testimonies for the Church* Vol. 8, p. 117.

Seal of God. In deciphering the meaning of Revelation, I needed to do so from a New Covenant perspective rather than the Old. It soon became clear that the Seal of God in the New Testament is not the Sabbath at all. In fact, the New Testament Scriptures are clear. The Seal of God is the Holy Spirit. In Ephesians 1 we read,

> In Him you also trusted, after you heard the word of truth, the gospel of your salvation; in whom also, having believed, you were *sealed* with the Holy Spirit of promise, who is the *guarantee* of our inheritance until the redemption of the purchased possession, to the praise of His glory. Eph 1:13-14

Ephesians 4:30-32 restates it this way:

> And do not grieve the Holy Spirit of God, by whom you were *sealed* for the day of redemption. Let all bitterness, wrath, anger, clamor, and evil speaking be put away from you, with all malice. And be kind to one another, tenderhearted, forgiving one another, just as God in Christ forgave you.

2 Corinthians 1:20-22 uses the same imagery:

> For all the promises of God in Him are Yes, and in Him Amen, to the glory of God through us. Now He who establishes us with you in Christ and has anointed us is God, who also has *sealed* us and given us the Spirit in our hearts as a *guarantee*.

To ignore these clear statements is to ignore what the New Testament plainly teaches. Revelation must be interpreted from the perspective of the Cross and the New Covenant. To insist on the Old Covenant definitions is to do injustice to the text.

Secondly, the word John uses for commandments (*entolé* in Greek) is never used in John's writings to refer to the Ten Commandments. When John is speaking of the law in general, or the Ten Commandments in particular, he always uses the Greek word *nomos* for law. When John uses *entolé* he does so in conjunction with the instructions of Jesus for practical love of one another. He never breaks this pattern.[3] So Revelation 12:17 is not speaking about the Old Covenant Ten Commandments at all. We must be consistent in translating John's writings if we wish to arrive at his intended meaning. It became apparent to me that the SDA position had not only ignored the context of the New Testament for the Seal of God, but had missed the consistent use of the Greek language by the writer John. With this pattern clearly in mind, Revelation 12:17 is properly translated into English (in harmony with John's use of *entolé*) "those who truly love one another, and are telling the world about Jesus." To translate it to mean the observance of law, specifically Sabbath observance, is reading into the text preconceived ideas, rather than letting the text speak for itself.

The Holy Spirit according to John 13-16 is another Comforter. He lives in us and guides us. He is the indwelling Jesus in our lives. The Seal of God in the last days represents those who have a daily personal walk with Jesus through the agency of the Holy Spirit. This is what it means to be sealed. When we receive the gift of the Holy Spirit by receiving Jesus, we enter the daily rest experience of God's amazing grace. This is the same message as found in Hebrews 3-4. When we are resting in Jesus today and every day, He is our Sabbath. The Spirit is the guarantee of our inheritance! (Eph. 4:14) In short, the Seal of God is Jesus living in us through the agency of the Holy Spirit.

---

[3]Dale Ratzlaff, *Sabbath in Crisis* (Glendale, AZ, 1990) pp 310-311.

The "mark of the beast," in contrast, would be for those who choose to *not* believe, or refuse to accept the gift of grace, refuse to rest in Jesus, and choose rather to depend on another way. Those who choose to depend on their own works instead of trusting in God's only Son will receive the "mark of the beast."

CHAPTER TWELVE

THE SABBATH IN THE GOSPELS

I had spent much time in the application section of the New Testament: the Epistles, Acts, and Revelation. It became clear that there is no continued binding requirement for keeping the seventh-day Sabbath. What comes through loud and clear in the New Testament Epistles is that Jesus fulfilled the Sabbath. The day-ness has been, at the very least, de-emphasized. It is *not* to be used as a dividing issue or binding command for Gentile Christians. It is not to be seen as a test of loyalty. Instead, a daily walk with Jesus through the agency of the Holy Spirit is the new *seal* or *test*.

The next question I needed to ask was, "What did Jesus teach, and what significance did He place on the Sabbath?" I remembered that Jesus came as one under the Law to redeem those under the Law, (Gal. 4:4-5) so He had to live under all of the Law's requirements. At the same time, I needed to see whether he taught and lived in such a way as to set the stage for a fulfillment motif, or taught a continuance theology. I began in Matthew 5 where Jesus says,

> Do not think that I came to destroy the Law or the Prophets. I did not come to destroy but to fulfill. For assuredly, I say to you, till heaven and earth pass away, one jot or one tittle will by no means pass from the law till all is fulfilled. Matt. 5:17-18.

This is a text that I used to quote when trying to prove that the Sabbath was still binding. At first glance, this text does seem to indicate that the continuance theory is correct in Jesus' teaching. It does seem to say that the Law is an eternal institution. But a closer examination reveals otherwise. First, I noticed the phrase, "Law and Prophets." Jesus is not referring to the Ten Commandment Law here specifically. He is using the word *nomos* to refer to the entire first five books of Moses. "The Prophets" refers to the rest of the Old Testament. So this is not a specific reference to the Ten Commandments at all. If one "jot" or one "tittle" cannot pass from the Law, we cannot pick and choose which laws are permanent and which are not. The whole Old Testament is still binding in every tiny detail. For example, we must not mix one type of cloth with another, we must execute Sabbath-breakers, and we must not have relations with our spouses until at least seven days after the woman's period ends. We must sacrifice animals, must stay outside until evening if we have touched a football (pigskin is unclean!) and much more. The list could go on and on. By the way, you must not mix milk products with beef (a Quarter Pounder with cheese is a sin). If you touch a dead carcass you must be quarantined. All of the religious feasts still apply. Is that what Jesus is saying? Are we still under Law until Heaven and earth pass away? Are all these things still binding? *No*! The key word to understanding this passage is the word "*fulfilled*." Jesus is saying that no part of the Law can be ignored, not even the least stroke of a pen, even if heaven and earth pass away. You can't do it yourself or teach others to do so, until all is *fulfilled*!

If you read through the book of Matthew and through each of the Gospels the word "*fulfilled*" is repeated over and over. Get an exhaustive concordance and check it out. Here are a few examples. Matthew 1:22-23 refers to the fulfillment of the prophecy about the virgin being with child. Matthew 2:15 discusses the prophecy that he would be called out of Egypt. Matthew 8:17 is about the fulfilled prophecy concerning His healing ministry. The list goes on and on. Finally, after finding this recurring theme through each Gospel account, we come to John 19 where we find these words:

> After this, Jesus, knowing that all things were now accomplished, that the Scripture might be *fulfilled,* said, "I thirst!" Now a vessel full of sour wine was sitting there; and they filled a sponge with sour wine, put it on hyssop, and put it to His mouth. So when Jesus had received the sour wine, He said, "It is finished!" And bowing His head, He gave up His spirit.

Jesus did not come to destroy but to "*fulfill.*" Jesus came to be the fulfillment of all the Old Covenant laws, ceremonies, rituals, and symbols. These were a shadow or prefiguring of what was to come. To my surprise this fulfillment motif fit perfectly with what I had learned repeatedly throughout the Epistles and the rest of the application section of the New Testament. There was no contradiction at all! So I kept reading and came to this intriguing verse, Matthew 11:28-30, where Jesus calls Himself the rest provider. "*Come to Me, all you who labor and are heavy laden, and I will give you rest.*"

Jesus then encourages His followers to take His *yoke* upon them. (Remember what Acts 15 and Galatians 5 call the Law: *a yoke of bondage too heavy to bear.*) Here Jesus discusses His way of freedom and rest. Jesus appears to be contrasting Himself with the Law. The way of relationship with Himself is the easy and restful way.

Is this mere speculative thinking? Is there any connection with this statement by Jesus and the Law, specifically the Sabbath? Notice the very next verses. There can be no confusion as to what He was referring. Jesus' discussion goes directly to the issue of the Sabbath. Notice the following verses, and remember there were no chapter and verse separations in the original Scripture.

> At that time Jesus went through the grain fields on the Sabbath. And His disciples were hungry, and began to pluck heads of grain and to eat. And when the Pharisees saw it, they said to Him, "Look, Your disciples are doing what is not lawful to do on the Sabbath!" But He said to them, "Have you not read what David did when he was hungry, he and those who were with him: how he entered the house of God and ate the showbread which was not lawful for him to eat, nor for those who were with him, but only for the priests? Or have you not read in the law that on the Sabbath the priests in the temple profane the Sabbath, and are blameless? Yet I say to you that in this place there is One greater than the temple. But if you had known what this means, "I desire mercy and not sacrifice," you would not have condemned the guiltless. For the Son of Man is Lord even of the Sabbath. Mt. 12:1-8

Immediately after Jesus' statement about taking His yoke of rest we find this statement. Jesus specifically sets up a Sabbath debate. Now some might argue that Jesus did not set this up, it was the religious leaders who set it up. But the use of the word "*time*" makes it clear that this debate was set up by Jesus. The word for time in the original Greek is the word "c*hairos*" not "c*hronos*." The latter word refers to chronological time or ordinary course of time. But the word "*chairos*" is a word used for opportune time. It could more accurately be translated "at that moment of opportunity," or "at that teachable moment." Jesus leads his disciples through a grain field knowing their usual habit of eating grain when hungry to set up this teachable moment. It is in this context that Jesus responds to the religious leaders' accusations with some fascinating teaching.

Notice the following points that Jesus makes as His disciples get stopped by the religious patrol for working on the Sabbath. This was not an infraction of the Mosaic code, only of some of the Rabbinic traditions, but it is interesting to see how Jesus answers the accusations. First He tells the story of David and how he, the anointed king to be, asked for showbread to eat from the sanctuary. This was not a lawful thing to do, but since he was on king's business he did so without being guilty. The question I asked myself was, "What type of law was David breaking? Was it the moral or ceremonial law?" Was this law that David broke of the type of law that had eternal moral value, or was it of the category of specific temporary religious significance? It was the temporary ceremonial law of course. David was not exempt from moral laws. We know that when he broke the seventh commandment and committed adultery with Bathsheba there was a severe price to pay.

Next, notice in verse 5, Jesus reminds the Pharisees that the priests in the temple can break the Sabbath while doing their priestly duties. The priests have an exemption from the Sabbath law while carrying out religious functions. Now I asked myself again, under which category of commandments does this priestly office fall? The priestly system is clearly under the ceremonial system. It was part of the specific religious system of the Old Covenant. Were the priests exempt from the moral commands? Could they lie, cheat, steal, commit adultery? No, of course they could not. I remembered that this same basic argument was used by Jesus in John 7:22-23. There

Jesus says to his accusers that the Law of Moses regarding circumcision takes precedence over the Sabbath. If the day to be circumcised happened to be the Sabbath, the circumcision was carried out. Now I asked myself again, "With which category of law is the Sabbath placed in each of these scenarios?" The ceremonial! In each case Jesus places it with the temporary or ceremonial rules and restrictions, not the moral absolutes of all time. He even states this one more time when He says:

> But if you had known what this means, "I desire mercy and not sacrifice," you would not have condemned the guiltless. Mt. 12:7

One more time Jesus contrasts the temporary system "sacrifice" with the eternal moral absolute of "mercy." The Sabbath is classified with the temporary ceremonial system every time. In what category does this place Sabbath? Ceremonial shadows of course! Jesus is saying to the accusers, "If David could eat showbread (breaking a ceremonial law), if the priests could do work in the temple on Sabbath, if circumcision could be carried out on the Sabbath, if Sabbath is part of the sacrificial system not the eternal moral principles, then the Anointed One, the Son of Man, surely is Lord of the Sabbath. He is over and above these ceremonial regulations.

I must admit that this discovery affected me deeply. Jesus Himself placed the Sabbath with the things that we know now were shadows of what was to come. He placed the Sabbath with the ceremonial system. He set the stage for Colossians 2:17, where it clearly states that the entire Sabbath system was a "shadow of things to come, but the substance (reality) is Christ." Jesus, prior to the Cross, was already teaching the New Covenant. What I had been taught in the sabbatarian educational system had completely passed over Jesus' intent in this passage. Jesus' pre-Cross teaching fits exactly with what He revealed to

Paul in the book of Galatians, in Colossians 2:16-17, and elsewhere in the Epistles.

In Mark two we find this story repeated. Mark 2:27 adds one statement, however. "The Sabbath was made for man and not man for the Sabbath." Some Adventist scholars say this means that it was established at Creation and therefore a moral ought and binding for all time. But the problem with that interpretation is the linguistics study does not bear this out. Jesus is not making a universal statement here. He is basically saying that the Sabbath was made for man, not the other way around. The context teaches that Sabbath is not in the category of moral oughts. It is lumped in with the temporary or ceremonial system. This truth, right from the heart of Jesus' Sabbath teachings, truly opened up to me a new paradigm. I had always studied these passages with the agenda of showing that Sabbath must be the Lord's Day. (Therefore the statement in Revelation 1:10 regarding the Lord's Day must refer to the seventh-day Sabbath and not to Sunday). While doing that, I had missed the intended message from the passage. Jesus was plainly setting the stage for a fulfillment theology.

One more observation—the passage in Matthew begins with Jesus calling Himself the Rest Provider. Mark's account starts with this statement:

> And no one puts new wine into old wineskins; or else the new wine bursts the wineskins, the wine is spilled, and the wineskins are ruined. But new wine must be put into new wineskins. Mk. 2:22

In Luke's account of the same story, the same introduction is used. (Luke. 5:36-39) Jesus is teaching (the Gospel writers understood it) that it is not possible to hang onto the old system and at the same time make room for the true Sabbath, Jesus Christ. One or the other will have to give. No, Jesus does not directly say that the Sabbath will no longer be a binding issue in the new era, but He does endorse it fully by what He taught and modeled. He clearly points to Himself as the fulfillment and warns against letting the form cause us to miss the true Sabbath, Himself.

Another illustration from the Gospels that deeply impacted me, because I had never noticed it before, is found in Luke 4:16. To set the background, a knowledge of the Sabbath system in the Old Testament is essential. Starting in Leviticus 23-25 the system is laid out. It starts with the weekly Sabbaths that point forward to the monthly and yearly festivals, which in turn point forward to the sabbatical years, which point forward to the ultimate Sabbath, the year of Jubilee. After the seventh sabbatical was celebrated, in the 50th year, there was to be a year of Jubilee when all the land was to be returned to original owners, all the slaves were to be freed, all the indentured servants were considered debt free. It was a year of freedom. It was this Jubilee that was referred to in Isaiah 61:1-2 in reference to the coming Messiah. He was to usher in the ultimate Jubilee. Now with that backdrop notice how Luke 4:16ff reads:

> So He came to Nazareth, where He had been brought up, And as His custom was, He went into the synagogue on the Sabbath day, and stood up to read. And He was handed the book of the prophet Isaiah. And when He had opened the book, He found the place where it was written: "The Spirit of the Lord is upon Me, because He has anointed Me to preach the gospel to the poor; He has sent me to heal the brokenhearted, to proclaim liberty (preach deliverance) to the captives and recovery of sight to the blind, to set at liberty those who are oppressed; to proclaim (preach) the acceptable year of the Lord." Then He closed the book, and gave it to the attendant and sat down. And the eyes of all who were in the synagogue were fixed on Him. And

He began to say to them, "Today this Scripture is *fulfilled* in your hearing." Luke 4:16-21

Jesus not only claimed to be the Messiah in this statement, but He called himself the *Jubilee*! Jesus called Himself the *Ultimate Sabbath*! He was claiming to be the Messiah and the Sabbath personified. The people knew exactly what He was claiming! They tried to kill Him for it. Can Jesus be any more clear about who He is? The Sabbath is a Person![1]

I became even more excited as I read the verses and the chapters that followed. Jesus cast out demons, healed the sick, cleansed lepers, and forgave sins, all *Jubilee activities*! Finally, on the second Sabbath, as He was going through the grainfields plucking and eating grain, the Pharisees showed up. Jesus was doing what was part of the instruction on how people were to eat during the year of Jubilee! Eat out of the fields! As I read all of these things, it was like the blinders were falling off of my eyes. I was seeing a Jesus who was making an intentional claim to be the Sabbath personified.

The Gospel of John relates a story that underscores this understanding. In John 5 we read the story of the man Jesus healed by the pool of Bethesda. He instructed the man to "rise, take up his bed, and walk." The religious leaders are particularly disturbed by this because it is in direct violation of the Old Covenant Sabbath laws. It is also problematic for modern day sabbatarians because here Jesus commands a man to break a biblical law, not a Rabbinic law. The Old Covenant was clear that carrying a burden on the Sabbath was strictly forbidden and punishable by death.[2] Yet Jesus ignores this and actually commands the man to ignore it as well. The religious

---

[1] Clay Peck, *New Covenant Christians* (Grace Place publications, Berthoud Colorado, 1998) pp 79-88.

[2] See Numbers 15:32-36, Nehemiah 13:19, and Jeremiah 17:21-22.

leaders quickly began to verbally attack Jesus for His work on the Sabbath and His encouragement of the man to do so as well. In reply, Jesus called attention to His Father and His work on the Sabbath. Since His Father worked on the Sabbath, Jesus stated that it was appropriate for Him to do so as well. Notice the response of the leaders in John 5:

> Therefore the Jews sought all the more to kill Him, because *He not only broke the Sabbath, but also said that God was His Father, making Himself equal with God.* John. 5:18

This passage of Scripture was recorded by John sometime around 90 A.D. He does not argue with the statement but lists it as fact. We would all agree that Jesus called Himself equal with God. Did he not also break the Sabbath? According to the Old Testament Scripture He did. According to John's record He did as well. John did not say "they thought He broke the Sabbath", or "He broke their idea of what Sabbath should be." He stated that the reason they wanted to kill Him was because *He broke the Sabbath.*[3]

If Jesus had *already fulfilled* all that the Sabbath pointed forward to, as we just studied in Luke 4:18ff. then He was at complete liberty to ignore the Sabbath regulations and to teach others to do so. On the other hand, if He had not, then He was guilty of breaking the Sabbath and teaching others to do so. What does that imply as it relates to Matthew 5:17-19? There Jesus said that the one who breaks the least of the commandments and teaches others to follow suit would be called least in God's kingdom. These are the only alternatives. Either Jesus was the fulfillment of the Sabbath, therefore at total liberty to ignore and teach others to ignore these Sabbath regulations,

---

[3] Richard Fredericks, *The Sabbath in Christ* (Sermon series presented at Damascus Road Community Church, Damascus MD, 1999) Part 1.

or He was Himself guilty of Sabbath breaking and encouraging others to step outside of God's will. This would have disqualified Him from being our Savior and our perfect Substitute. The former explanation is the only one that makes sense.

Finally, the story of the Transfiguration began to have new significance for me. You remember how Moses and Elijah appeared on top of the mountain with Jesus as He was transfigured (Matthew 17). I always thought that this was a miniature picture of the Kingdom, but I missed an important statement made by God. Moses, to the people of that day, represented the Law, the first five books. Often the Law was just referred to as Moses. The ultimate prophet in the Old Testament era according to the Jews was Elijah. He represented the prophets to them. These were highly significant figures to the Jewish people. They represented to them the entire revelation of God up to that point.

It was at this point that Peter suggested that they remain there and the disciples would build three shelters for the three to be together in that place. He is in essence saying that Elijah and Moses and Jesus are all on the same level. We have Moses here, we have Elijah here, and we have Jesus too! Now we have all of the revelation of God past, present and future -- Right? Wait a minute! Suddenly a bright cloud overshadowed them and a voice from the cloud said, "This is My beloved Son, in whom I am well pleased, *hear Him*!" (Mt 17:5) The disciples were terrified, of course, but after a while they looked up. What did they see? They saw *Jesus alone.* I had never seen the significance of this before. Jesus and the Law and the Prophets are standing side by side. God says, "Listen to My Son!" It is not the Law and the Prophets *and* Jesus. For the Christian era, it is *only Jesus*. Jesus is in a league all by Himself. He is the clearest revelation of God. The Law and the Prophets have their place, but fade into insignificance next to Jesus. This verse helped to underscore in my mind the teaching of Galatians, Romans and the rest of the Epistles, that the final authority now is not the Law or Prophets, but Jesus.[4] Notice Hebrews 1:1-3:

> God, who at various times and in various ways spoke in time past to the fathers by the prophets, *has in these last days spoken to us by His Son*, whom He has appointed heir of all things, through whom also He made the worlds; who *being the brightness of His glory and the express image of His person*, and upholding all things by the word of His power. . .

---

[4] Ibid, Part 1

CHAPTER THIRTEEN

SABBATH IN THE OLD TESTAMENT

After thorough study in the New Testament, it was time to go back to the Old Testament. I had always thought that Sabbath was established at Creation. Since Sabbath was a Creation ordinance, then it must be pre-Law, and should have a universal significance. So I went to Genesis two where the end of Creation is recorded.

> And on the seventh day God ended His work which He had done, and He rested on the seventh day from all His work which He had done. Then God blessed the seventh day and sanctified it, because in it He rested from all His work which God had created and made. Gen. 2:2-3

"There it is!" I thought to myself. "Sabbath was established at Creation. Since that is true, it must be a forever institution!" A problem soon emerged in my mind as I examined that initial conclusion. It seemed to require making too many assumptions. First, there is no "evening and morning" mentioned in this text. All the other Creation days conclude with the phrase "evening and morning." Each of the first six days concludes with a clear reference to this 24 hour time period. But the seventh day does not contain this phrase. I had to ask myself "Why the change? That is not to say that this was not a literal day, but there is a unique aspect of this day that is implied. This was no accident by the author. It was not an oversight by Moses. He was always careful to record in detail. So why was the "evening and morning" motif suddenly omitted? Could it be that God intended that the rest He had established would have a continuing quality? Could it be that it was intended that it would have remained as a daily experience had it not been for the incursion of sin? Would this rest have been a perpetual reality had it not been for sin?

Second, the word Sabbath is not mentioned. There is no mention of this being a Sabbath. In fact, we do not find the word Sabbath mentioned for at least 2,500 years. If this was the establishment of a required Sabbath observance, would it not have been called such? Would there not have been some command associated with it. We find the command for unity and faithfulness in marriage clearly given in Genesis 2:24.

Third, there was no need for Adam and Eve to rest because they had not worked. This was clearly a reference to God's *rest*, or stopping His act of creating. He rested or ceased from creating and blessed the day and set it apart. This could have been a one time day of blessed celebration. There is no indication that this was to be a weekly ritual or event.

Finally, there is no record that anyone ever kept the Sabbath from that time until God taught the people about it in the wilderness. It is first mentioned after they were delivered from Egypt. The marriage institution, on the other hand, is mentioned repeatedly throughout that entire time period. There is much evidence of it being part of the way of life during those years. But there is no mention of the Sabbath for 2500 years! It is highly unlikely that the Sabbath would never have been mentioned during this time if it truly was established at Creation. What I learned from a closer examination of the Creation account is that the Creation ordinance idea has some serious weaknesses. So if I was going to be faithful to what the text actually says, I had to admit that two interpretations are feasible: 1) a Creation ordinance of a seventh-day Sabbath, or 2) a completed work and celebration that was intended to affect the world for every day thereafter. The latter meaning would indicate that God never intended for humans to toil in hardship to make it in life. There was to be a perpetual state of rest in unbroken relationship with the Creator.

We do not find Sabbath mentioned again until Exodus 16:23. God explains the Sabbath concept to the people of Israel through the manna experience. As I studied, it became evident that the people were unaware of any Sabbath up to this time. They had been given some new commandments, such as the sacrifice of the lamb in Exodus 12, and the institution of the Passover feast in the same time period. They knew about circumcision, but they had not yet been introduced to the Sabbath. The context is clear that the people had to be taught about the Sabbath.

The Sabbath is later expanded into one of the Ten Commandments in Exodus 20:8-11. There they were instructed to *remember* the Sabbath. Some have suggested that this refers to Creation establishment, others that it refers to the manna episode. Either interpretation is feasible in the text. Notice that those who were obligated to rest included "the stranger within your gates," a different group from the "stranger that sojourns among you" in Leviticus 17-18. This command was not for everyone as a Creation ordinance might indicate. (See comments on Acts 15 in the previous chapter.) Finally, verse 11 reads:

> For in six days the Lord made the heavens and the earth, the sea, and all that is in them, but He rested on the seventh day. Therefore the Lord blessed the Sabbath day and made it holy. Ex. 20:11 (NIV)

Now again, at first glance this seems to indicate that this was a Creation ordinance that had been established at Creation. And the text definitely allows for that. But it also allows for the other notion that since God is Creator you are to worship Him as such. His blessing and sanctification of the seventh day at Creation is now, since the manna instruction, being called the Sabbath, the Sabbath part of the institution being established here in Exodus 16. God has the right to demand this of His followers because they are His created beings. Again, two possible interpretations are permissible here; a Creation ordinance, or a later establishment by the same Creator in the manna incident.

One additional point needs to be addressed. The first five books of the Bible are all attributed to Moses according to the New Testament. Therefore, was Moses speaking from the vantage point of the Law when He wrote the following in Genesis? Was he writing after the Law had been given on Mount Sinai?

> Thus the heavens and the earth, and all the host of them, were finished. And on the seventh day God ended His work which He had done, and He rested on the seventh day from all His work which He had done. Then God blessed the seventh day and sanctified it, because in it He rested from all His work which God had created and made. Gen. 2:1-3

If I am traveling through Texas and I ask for the directions to President Bush's birth place, the people will assume that I know that George W. Bush was not president when he was born. I call him President Bush from my vantage point. Bible writers had a vantage point for their writing as well. As we studied earlier, Mark's Gospel makes a comment about clean and unclean foods based on Jesus' discussion with the Pharisees. Jesus did not state directly that the food laws were going to be obsolete, but Mark, from his vantage point after the Cross applies it that way. Was this Genesis account one of those after-the-fact statements based on Moses' vantage point? Was Moses writing to the Children of Israel about God blessing and setting apart the seventh day from their perspective or vantage point? If so, the fact that the name "Sabbath" was omitted is even more significant.

Since either the creation ordinance of the Sabbath or the later ordinance interpretation honor the text, I needed to study further to see if the context of the Old Testament gives a clue as to which is correct. What deeply impacted me was the clarity of the other texts on this subject. They state exactly which way to interpret these texts. There is no need for confusion. We don't have to speculate as to whether Moses was writing from the post-Law vantage point or not. One thing I have found in my studies, on important issues God always provides at least three or more Scriptures to make sure we are not led astray.[1] He does not

---

[1] This is one reason the Adventist doctrine of the investigative judgment is so shaky in my opinion. It is based on one text that comes from an obscure passage of apocalyptic literature. It is complicated by the fact that the immediate context does not appear to be talking about a heavenly but an earthly issue. It is connected to other Scripture by the weakest of linguistic ties, and it ignores the actual wording of the evening and morning sacrificial imagery within the text. In order to make the horn power of Daniel 8 fit the Adventist scenario, one must make this horn grow out of one of the winds rather than the horns of the Grecian empire where it logically fits. The obvious connection to Antiochus Epiphanes is ignored. To base an entire doctrine on such a stretch is highly suspect. There are no biblical scholars outside of Adventism who agree with the SDA interpretation. This ought to throw up a caution sign for making too many dogmatic claims. Essentially the SDA position has one weak text and Ellen G. White for support. That doesn't sound like the Bible and the Bible only to me.

leave us to guess, or to be *super-smart* or *gifted* to understand what is really important. One text that brought clarification on the Sabbath issue for me was Exodus 31:12ff.

> And the Lord spoke to Moses saying, "Speak also to the *children of Israel,* saying: "Surely My Sabbaths you shall keep, for it is a *sign between Me and you* throughout *your* generations, that you may know that I am the Lord who sanctifies you. You shall keep my Sabbath, therefore, for it is *holy to you.* Everyone who profanes it shall surely be put to death; . . . Therefore the *children of Israel* shall keep the Sabbath, to observe the Sabbath throughout their generations as a perpetual covenant. It is *a sign between me and the children of Israel* forever; for in six days the Lord made the heavens and the earth, and on the seventh day He rested and was refreshed." And when He had made an end of speaking with him on Mount Sinai, He gave Moses the Two tablets of the Testimony, tablets of stone, written with the finger of God. Ex. 31:12-18

Notice how plain this is. The Sabbath was between God and Israel and was placed on the table of the covenant with that relationship in mind. Deuteronomy 5:2-3 makes the same point.

> The Lord our God made a covenant with us in Horeb. *The Lord did not make this covenant with our fathers, but with us* who are here today, all of us who are alive.

The text goes on to reiterate the Ten Commandments including the fourth, but this time the reason for keeping the Sabbath is because God delivered them from the Egyptians. The Deuteronomy account is a reference to Israel only, and one that was not established before the Exodus, but was a sign of the rest provided by that deliverance event. Nehemiah confirms this interpretation once again:

> You came down also on Mount Sinai, and spoke with them from heaven, and gave them just ordinances and true laws, good statutes and commandments. *You made known to them Your holy Sabbath*, and commanded them precepts, statutes and laws, by the hand of Moses Your servant. Neh. 9:13-14

Ezekiel 20:10-12 conveys the same understanding:

> Therefore I made them go out of the land of Egypt and brought them into the wilderness. And I gave them My statutes and showed them My judgments, which if a man does, he shall live by them. Moreover *I also gave them My Sabbaths, to be a sign between them and Me,* that they might know that I am the Lord who sanctifies them.

These Scriptures could not be more definitive regarding the time of the establishment of the Sabbath. These passages remove all ambiguity about the time and location of the Sabbath command. Each one places the Sabbath right in the heart of the covenant with Israel and was to be between them and God. It was *not* a Creation ordinance as I had been taught to believe. It is not binding on all people for all time. This again agreed with what I had learned in the New Testament. The entire message of the Bible fits together. The Sabbath was a day established by God as a covenant between Himself and Israel. Jesus came to fulfill the Law and to be our Sabbath. Christians rest in the finished work of Christ as their Sabbath rest. As children of Abraham, Christians are counted righteous because of their faith, just as Abraham was before the Law or circumcision. The entire biblical picture is in agreement from beginning to end.

Some have tried to perpetuate the Sabbath institution, claiming that it is the only one of the Ten Commandments that has been forgotten, and yet it is the only one that commands the people to *remember*. True, the Sabbath command does start with the instruction *to remember the Sabbath day.* This was the remembrance or outward sign/seal of the Old Covenant. The entrance sign, we remember, was circumcision and the remembrance sign was Sabbath. But in the New Covenant, the entrance sign, according to Colossians 2:11-12, is baptism. What is the remembrance sign of the New Covenant? If Jesus is our Sabbath *rest*, what is the sign of this New Covenant *rest*? Notice 1 Corinthians 11:23-26:

> For I received from the Lord that which I also delivered to you: that the Lord Jesus on the same night in which He was betrayed took bread; and when He had given thanks, He broke it and said, "Take, eat; this is My body which is broken for you; *do this in remembrance of Me*." In the same manner He also took the cup after supper, saying, "This cup is the new covenant in My blood. This do, as often as you drink it, *in remembrance of Me*. For as often as you eat this bread and drink this cup, you proclaim the Lord's death till He comes."

The remembrance sign of the New Covenant is the Lord's Supper. As often as we do this we do so in remembrance of Jesus. Jesus is the sign of the New Covenant. The Seal of God is the indwelling of the Holy Spirit through whom Jesus lives in us![2] The Lord's Supper sign is not attached to a day or time either. Jesus told us that we demonstrate the remembrance of the New Covenant *as often as we do this*. Notice the following Scripture from Isaiah 49:8 predicting the Messiah:

---

[2] Dale Ratzlaff, *Sabbath in Crisis* (Glendale, AZ, 1990) pp 182-186.

> Thus says the LORD: "In an acceptable time I have heard You, and in the day of salvation I have helped You; I will preserve You and give *You as a covenant* to the people, to restore the earth, to cause them to inherit the desolate heritages."

Jesus Himself is the covenant! Isaiah predicted that the Messiah Himself would be the covenant. In the Old Covenant, Sabbath was the sign, or the essence of the covenant. In the New Covenant, it is Jesus! Symbolically, His body and blood are the remembrance sign and may be celebrated anytime, anywhere. It reminds us that Jesus Himself is the New Covenant. Notice how Luke 2:10-12 uses the word *sign*. I do not believe this was a mere coincidence. Notice carefully the wording of this verse of scripture.

> Then the angel said to them, "Do not be afraid, for behold, I bring you good tidings of great joy which will be to all people. For there is born to you this day in the city of David a Savior, who is Christ the Lord. And this will be *the sign to you*: You will find a Babe wrapped in swaddling cloths, lying in a manger."

In Luke 2:33-35 Simeon, an elderly prophetic man of God, uses the same word, *sign,* in his prophecy concerning Jesus.

> And Joseph and His mother marveled at those things which were spoken of Him. Then Simeon blessed them, and said to Mary His mother, "Behold, this Child is destined for the fall and rising of many in Israel, and *for a sign* which will be spoken against (yes, a sword will pierce through your own soul also), that the thoughts of many hearts may be revealed."

Jesus is the sign of the New Covenant. He is the covenant! The communion service is the outward celebration of the New Covenant and the *seal* of that covenant is the Holy Spirit dwelling in us! Scriptures are clear once again.

CHAPTER FOURTEEN

ADVENTIST STICKING POINTS

Now that the message of the Bible on the Sabbath had been studied and the teaching clear to my mind, there were some sticking points that seemed to contradict this consistent theme. One example of this is the statement that Adventists often quote to imply that everyone in the new earth will be keeping the seventh-day Sabbath.

> "For as the new heavens and the new earth which I will make shall remain before Me," says the LORD, "So shall your descendants and your name remain. And it shall come to pass that from one New Moon to another, and from one Sabbath to another, all flesh shall come to worship before Me," says the LORD. Is. 66:22-23

Adventists teach that this is proof that the Sabbath is an eternal institution and is, therefore, still binding today. So I went to that passage to read it for myself and discovered a few interesting facts. One, the text states that the celebrations will be "from one New Moon to another and from one Sabbath to another." Does this mean that New Moon festivals are unchangeable and eternal? Will they be required in the next life? Should they be kept today? Are they still binding? Then I noticed that the next couple of verses speak about the inhabitants walking around and encountering the dead bodies of those who have rebelled against the Lord. That didn't sound like the new earth as described in Revelation. In reading the larger context of the same vision, I found "for the child will die one hundred years old." (Isaiah 65:20) What a strange picture of heaven--dead bodies of the enemies of God encountered as one walks around the city, and people dying after 100 years or so! The reason it sounds so strange is because the "new heavens and new earth" that Isaiah is talking about is not the new earth of Revelation where "there will be no more death or sorrow or crying." Instead, it is describing Isaiah's picture of what the earth would have been like if Israel had accepted the Messiah and become the center attraction of the world. People would have come to Israel to see what their God had done. They would have joined Israel in worship and God's blessings would have made this earthly "New Jerusalem" the center of the world. This prediction was one of those prophecies that was conditional on the acceptance of the Messiah. Since Israel rejected the Messiah, it was not fulfilled.

Another sticking question for Adventists is Jesus' statement telling his disciples to pray that their "flight may not be in the winter or on the Sabbath" (Mt 24:20). Doesn't this indicate that the Sabbath is still to be binding in the Christian era? The answer to that question came to light for me in reading Nehemiah 13, where Nehemiah was instituting some regulations concerning the business activities people were conducting on the Sabbath. Some of the surrounding Gentiles were bringing in their wares to sell to the Israelites on the Sabbath. This had been a snare for Israel before, had caused them to turn away from God, and eventually be taken into captivity. So Nehemiah made this regulation and it was still in effect in Jesus' day:

> So it was, at the gates of Jerusalem, as it began to be dark before the Sabbath, that I commanded the gates to be shut, and charged that they must not be opened 'till after the Sabbath. Neh. 13:19

In Matthew 24 Jesus' instruction was that the Christians were to be ready to make their escape as soon as they saw the Roman army pull back. This was to be their sign to escape. The Roman army would lift siege only for a short time. The rest of the inhabitants would be thinking that the armies had given up and go back to business as usual. But the Christians were to see this as their opportunity to escape. They were to pray, however, that it not be in winter for obvious reasons, and not on the Sabbath, because why? Sabbath would still be a binding institution? *No!* It was not considered by the Jews that running from danger, or even fighting in self defense during a time of war, was breaking the Sabbath command.[1] That was not the issue at all. The concern Jesus had for His followers, was that the gates of the city would be shut for the Sabbath and it would make the Christian escape virtually impossible. Jesus did not want His disciples to be trapped in the city when it was time to escape. Nehemiah's command helped me see how this fit together. Once again, the whole picture made perfect sense.

Another question that I wrestled with concerned the moral requirements for Christians. It seemed to me that the rest of the commandments in the Decalogue are still applicable for Christians, even though Romans and Galatians and the rest of the Epistles do teach that we are not under Law. The New Testament does encourage morality. Most Christians do emphasize keeping the commandments, all except the fourth. That seemed a little inconsistent to me. But in studying further, the answer

---

[1] Intertestamental literature bears this out as can be seen in the historical records of 1 Maccabees chapter 2.

became clear. Throughout the New Testament application section of the Bible (post-Cross) there are restatements of all of the moral "oughts" of the Ten Commandment Law, including some of the other Old Testament laws. However, these restatements *never* appeal to Law as the reason to observe them, but in every situation the appeal is to Christ. In Corinthians 6:18-20 for example, there is a clear admonition to sexual purity. It does *not,* however, use the Law as the reason for it, but rather that we are God's temple and the Spirit of Christ is in us. How could we join Jesus to a prostitute? The same pattern is found throughout the Epistles. Philippians 2 encourages kindness and love for one another, but does not appeal to Law. Instead it points us to the example of Jesus, who left heaven to die for us. With the example of Jesus' sacrifice, how can we but serve one another?

It is important to remember that the Epistles were especially written to *apply* the significance of the Christ event to Christians. I was completely amazed to discover that all of the commandments are restated as important for Christians in their relationship with Christ, except one--the Sabbath. Sabbath is *never* taught as a moral ought for Christians. Not once! Instead it is recognized as a daily *rest* in Jesus, as we have found in our study thus far. Notice the following summary of commandments restated in the New Testament:

1st Worship God only — at least 50 times

2nd No Idolatry — 12 times

3rd No profanity — 4 times

4th Remember Sabbath — no instructions given

5th Honor parents — 6 times

6th Don't murder — 6 times

7th No Adultery — 12 times

8th No stealing — 4 times

9th No lying — 4 times

10th Don't covet — 9 times[2]

If the Adventist position that the Sabbath will be the ultimate test of all time, is true, if it will one day be the final test of loyalty, if all true followers of Jesus will be keeping it, if all who fail to do so will receive the "mark of the beast," wouldn't it make sense that God would state it clearly? Wouldn't He repeatedly include it in His list of moral "oughts" for Christians throughout the New Testament? Wouldn't God warn and re-warn his disciples? Wouldn't Sabbath breaking be included in the lists of sins that Paul and the other New Testament writers stated and restated so many times in their warnings to the new believers? Why are there no instructions to "Jonas and Janeius Gentile" about how to keep the Sabbath? Wouldn't God have seen to it that the instructions were clear and precise as they are with the other nine commandments? Wouldn't there have been at least some questions about *how* to keep Sabbath in the Gentile world? Why would the apostles just assume that they would know how to observe Sabbath?

In my many years as an Adventist pastor, one of the most common questions I was asked by new converts and long standing members alike was, "What is OK and what is not OK to do on Sabbath?[3] How can we do this right? How

[2]J. Mark Martin, *The Sabbath: Common Misunderstandings,* Article posted on website www.sdaoutreach.org.

[3] Where to draw the line on Sabbath keeping issues has been a problem for many sabbatarians. Many Adventist boarding schools years ago, did not allow showers to be taken on the Sabbath. I grew up with certain unwritten rules regarding Sabbath observance. It was OK to wade on Sabbath, but not to swim. It was OK to ride bicycles, but not if there

do we know what to allow our kids to do on the holy day?" I cannot fathom that there would be *no instruction at all* on this issue during the Christian church era. It just does not make sense that such instruction would be left out, especially if eternal salvation could be affected by it. "Why?" is a reasonable question to ask of those who insist that Sabbath is the ultimate test of loyalty. The reason for the absence of such instruction is clear. Jesus is our Sabbath. Rest in Him each day, as we come to Him in faith, *is the Sabbath* of the New Testament. There is no other reasonable explanation.

Imagine that you are riding in a car with a friend at 25 miles per hour through your city. You are happy that your driver is careful to follow the speed limits while you are a passenger. You are grateful that he is safety conscious and law abiding. You don't think much of it until you pass out side the city limit sign and the speed limit changes to 35 mph and then to 50 and finally to 65, but your friend is still driving 25 miles per hour. Now you are beginning to wonder what is wrong. Cars are flying by, and the occupants are looking at you like you and your driver are

---

was a motor attached. It was OK to play games as long as "Bible" was part of the name. A Sabbath day's journey for us was the distance a person could travel on one tank of gas without refilling on the holy day. A person could eat in an Adventist cafeteria as long as Adventist script had been purchased the day before. The problem is clear. If the Old Testament law is still binding, then what business do we have allowing people to carry burdens, or travel, or prepare meals, or make all of these sub-rules? Is that any different from what the rabbis did with their 600+ Sabbath regulations? On the other hand, if the New Testament has reinterpreted these things in Christ, why not take what it says to its full and biblical conclusion and stop making Sabbath an issue at all? Shouldn't the focus be on Jesus, who is our true Sabbath? I realized that much of my Sabbath observance was really a neo-legalism with just another set of rules that our sub-system had set up. The New Testament silence on the issue of how to keep Sabbath makes a powerful statement that God did not intend for His followers to go down that road. (See Gal. 5:1) crazy or something. You wait a few minutes to make sure the car is not having mechanical problems or there is some other reason for this that you can't see. Finally you ask, "Do you mind telling me why you are driving 25 mph in a 65 mph zone?" Calmly yet firmly, your driver replies, "The sign in town said 25 miles per hour. I believe laws do not change. It would be fickle for my government to change like that. So I do not believe these other signs. I am sticking with the 25 mph law."

Sound ridiculous? Yes it does, but many sabbatarians do just that. They are quick to point out that God doesn't change. Therefore, if Sabbath was once required of God's people, then it must still be a permanent requirement. They disregard the other sign posts that clearly state otherwise. True, God's moral principles do not change. But the application of such principles often does. Just as the local city government follows the principle of safety in making speed limit laws, the application will be different in urban versus rural settings. The same is true with God's government. To insist on the *old* when the *new* has been clearly revealed, is to miss so much of the joy God has planned for His people.

CHAPTER FIFTEEN

WHAT ABOUT SUNDAY?

Well, what about Sunday worship? Is this right, wrong, or not an issue? My understanding from my study is that it is not an issue. It is neither right nor wrong. It is always right to worship God, in association with other believers as often as possible. In Acts 2:42-47 the early church was in worship everyday. If it were possible, such daily worship would be ideal. But we have busy lives to lead that make daily corporate worship impractical. Yet we need to have times for corporate worship to supplement our daily experience. We must not neglect corporate worship. (Heb. 10:25) It is not wrong to worship on Saturday and neither is it wrong to worship on Sunday, or Wednesday or any other day! Keeping a Sabbath for reflection and spiritual growth is healthy and should be encouraged. But the message of the New Testament, as well as the rest of the Bible, makes it clear that the day of the week on which worship takes place should *not* be binding or mandated for Christians.[1]

---

[1]Dale Ratzlaff, *Sabbath in Crisis*, Glendale, AR, 1990, pp 13-14. There are really three schools of thought in regard to the Sabbath. There is a small group, which includes the SDAs, that teach that the Sabbath has

There are those that make Sunday into a binding Sabbath requirement. As I understand the Scriptures, Sunday sabbatarianism is just as problematic as Saturday sabbatarianism. It is not wrong to observe a day. It is wrong to judge others for their decisions regarding observance or non-observance of days. It is wrong to, in any way, get such practices confused with salvation.

How did it happen that most Christians started worshipping on Sunday, then? It was interesting for me to discover the early church process with this. In an exhaustive study on the issue of Sabbath and Sunday, D.A. Carson, edits a book entitled *From Sabbath to the Lord's Day.* This book is a scholarly and highly technical work that examines the early church fathers and their views about Sabbath and Sunday worship.

From 100 A.D. forward the earliest Christians unanimously met on Sunday. This was a universal practice among Christians. No one considered it a Sabbath. But virtually all Christians met on that day. This historical reality is much earlier than Adventists have taught. These Sunday worship gatherings were universally accepted practice among the disciples of the apostles. It is unthinkable that this could have happened without having been the general practice during the apostolic era. Again I want to say that the early Christians thought it was a good day to meet because it celebrated the resurrection, but they did *not* associate it with a change of the seventh-day Sabbath. Some, however, continued to meet on the seventh-day Sabbath. These were mostly the Jewish Christians. Others, mostly Gentiles, did

---

continuance in the New Testament. A second group teaches a transference theology and states that the Sabbath command is still binding, but sacredness of the day was transferred from Sabbath to Sunday. (This was actually a much later development in the Christian church. Early Christians did not teach either of these first two concepts.) Finally there is a larger group of Christians that teach that Jesus fulfilled the Sabbath and the Law. He is our Sabbath rest.

not. They gave the reasons that we have previously discussed. Clearly, they understood the teachings of Paul and the rest of the Bible as we have just studied. The Sabbath was a permissible option, but not binding on Christians. However, there was a need to gather for corporate worship. Because many of the Jewish Christians would still attend synagogue on the Sabbath, there was a need to set aside another time when other Christians, including the Gentile Christians, could gather for their own private meetings. This became Sunday. Our first record of this reference was in 107 AD. That is only 11 years from the time of John's reference to the Lord's day in Revelation 1:10 It is quite probable that John was referring to Sunday when he mentioned that day—not because of any sacredness attached to it, but because it was the common meeting day for Christians.[2]

In 140 A.D. Justin Martyr held a detailed dialogue with Trypho, a Jewish critic of the Christians. In this debate he explains why the Christians do not observe any Sabbaths. He refers specifically to the Pauline Scriptures we have examined in this book. His arguments were based on the fulfillment of the Law in Christ, specifically the Sabbath. This detailed theological explanation to a Jewish critic clearly demonstrates how the early Christians believed. He was writing from the city of Ephesus where John had been the pastor/leader. This discussion took place only 44 years after the death of the Apostle and demonstrates what he considers to be the universal understanding of Christians at that time.[3] The idea that Sabbath was changed from Saturday to Sunday by the Catholic Church in later years is not borne out by the historical record.

The early Christians had some sentimental attachment to the first day of the week as well. Not only did the Lord rise on that day, but of the seven appearances of Jesus to his

---

[2] H. M. Riggle, *Sabbath and the Lord's Day*, (Glendale AZ: Life Assurance Ministries) pp. 114-135.

[3] Ibid. pp 121-130.

disciples, five were on the first day, and in the other appearances, there is no specific mention of which day they took place. Also that year, the feast of Pentecost was on the first day of the week. The Christian Church was born on a Sunday.[4] But this did *not* mean they attached sacredness or Sabbath qualities to that day. There were no appeals to the Ten Commandments attached to Sunday. Even much later when Constantine made the first Sunday Law, it was just a law to forbid work on that day, and it was a law that would benefit everyone. Pagans did not take Sunday off before that time. It was not a blending of Paganism and Christianity at all. It was a Christian day that Constantine used to benefit his empire. It was welcomed by Christians and Pagans alike as a break from work. It made worship more convenient, but *it was not a law based on Sabbath law at all.* In fact, *the farmers were exempt.* They could continue their work. This, of course, was strictly forbidden in the Old Covenant Sabbath laws, especially in the Ten Commandments. There was no changing of Sabbath to Sunday by Constantine as I had been taught.

There was some anti-Jewish sentiment at that time. Some have suggested that since the Jews were in trouble with the government, the Christians tried to distance themselves from the Jews by getting away from Sabbath so as to avoid persecution. But the records from that era do not indicate a people who did anything because they were trying to avoid persecution for the cause of Christ. The examples are myriad of Christians standing boldly for their faith in spite of the threat of death. If this had been a conviction for them, they would have stood for it. But they were *not* convicted about the Sabbath, as is clearly evident in their literature.

It was not until Augustine in the fifth century that any connection was made between the Ten Commandments and

[4] Ibid, pp. 142-143.

Sunday keeping. Even then the connection was loose. The day-ness of Sabbath was considered ceremonial. This view was made more prominent by Thomas Aquinas in later centuries. The reformers, Calvin and Luther, were careful to state that the Sabbath was not binding on Christians, but they saw merit in taking a day for rest and worship. It was not until the English Reformation that the Decalogue Sabbath began being promoted. The chief proponents of this were the Puritans. They began to teach that the Sabbath (although they called Sunday the Sabbath) was not abolished, and they instituted strict rules according to the Old Testament regulations. This, of course, affected the other religious English groups, such as the Methodists and the Baptists. Many of these groups came to America, and New England became known for strict Sabbath (Sunday) observance. It was there that one group, the Seventh-day Baptists, took it a step further and started keeping Saturday as the Sabbath. If the Old Testament Sabbath is binding on Christians, they reasoned, we should also keep the right day. It was the Seventh-day Baptists who influenced Joseph Bates, who in turn influenced Ellen G. White, and Seventh-day Adventism was born. Adventists are still primarily arguing with the "Puritans" over which day is the real Sabbath, rather than whether or not this is an issue in the New Testament for Christians. In arguing about which day is the Sabbath, the message of Scripture and the message the early church clearly had in mind, has been missed altogether.[5]

Is it wrong to keep a Saturday Sabbath? No, it is not. Romans 14:5-6 makes it clear that observing days or not

---

[5]D.A. Carson, *From Sabbath to the Lord's Day: A Biblical, Historical, and Theological Investigation* (Eugene OR, 1999) pp 221-341. This book, edited by Carson, details the history of Sunday observance and the theological understanding of the church from the time of the apostles to the present day. The SDA view of Sabbath and history does not stand up to the historical evidence.

observing days is not an issue. It is the judgmentalism associated with it that is forbidden. We must not judge one another over these things or make salvation issues out of them.

Imagine that you are on a business trip abroad for your job that has caused you to be separated from your family for several months. You miss your family and long for a meaningful time together even though you are apart. Your travel budget allows you to spend two hours once a week on the telephone with your family. So you set up a time when the whole family will gather around the telephone for this family communion. It becomes the highlight of your weekly schedule. Let's say that your family meets at home every Tuesday evening for your call, and it is early Wednesday morning for you where you are in the other country. Even so, this scheduled time is a wonderful and vital time for your family. Time flies by, and eventually you return home. It is so good to be back together! But do you keep on meeting every Tuesday evening now that you are back face-to-face? No. There is no longer need for a scheduled appointment now that you are face to face! However, if you choose to do so because this special family time became a special tradition while you were overseas, you might decide that you will keep the Tuesday evening date. Great idea! But now that you are back face to face all the time, is it mandatory that this weekly meeting happen? No, of course not! You might find another time works better for you. You might move it to Wednesday nights sometimes, or Friday nights. Maybe sometimes there could be several family meetings during the week. Now that you are back home face to face, it is not required that you meet at the same time in the same way. It is permissible, but not required.

The same is true of the weekly Sabbath. The Sabbath reminds us of God's original intent that we be human beings, not human doings. He created us for relationship with Himself. So it was in the days of old, the Sabbath pointed forward to the One who would come and restore that relationship with the Father. Every week the Children of Israel would physically rest to remind them of, and to point forward to these truths. But once Jesus came and restored that relationship with God and sent His Holy Spirit to live in us and to provide that continual *rest* relationship, we do not need to keep the day any more. It is ok to do so as long as no judgment is attached to keeping it. But it is *not* required. In the Old Covenant the Seal of God was the Sabbath, in the New, it is the Holy Spirit. Do you get the connection? Now we are not asked to remember Sabbath, but to remember Jesus. "In remembrance of Me," said Jesus.

I continued to pray in earnest about these things. Paula and I made this a subject of great soul searching and continued research. The whole study hit me so hard that I would wake up in the middle of the night and call out to God. "Lord, please do not let me be deceived. I want to be your faithful follower." I would go to the church very early in the morning during those months of intense study and prayer. Upstairs in the sanctuary of the church, I would sit down and play the piano and sing praises to the Lord. I privately called this my "Upper Room." It was the place I met God every day long before daylight and before anyone was around. There I would pour out all my fears and struggles to Jesus. Often I would weep and cry out from the very depths of my being. At times I would cry with deep sobs. There is no way to describe the anguish I felt. At times the fears of my youth were so intense that I would literally feel panic. What if I was wrong? What about all the dear people in the church. What if I led them astray and would be responsible for their being lost because I took a wrong turn. I experienced a sense of torture and agony during those days.

Every time, after much prayer and wrestling with God, the Scriptures would come to my mind with even greater clarity. I would claim Luke 11:11-13 over and over, day after day. Jesus says when we ask for the Holy Spirit, He will come to us. He will not send deception. Many times I would agonize with God and pray that He would lay me to rest rather than let me be deceived or let me dishonor His cause. The more I persisted, the more the Lord reassured me through His promises and His Word. Galatians 5:1 would come to mind with great clarity:

> Stand fast (firm), therefore in the liberty by which Christ has made us free, and do not be entangled again with a yoke of bondage.

This process went on for months. At times I would awake at 2:00 a.m. in a panic, terrified that I was going to be lost or would lead others astray. I would start pouring my heart out to the Lord and claiming His promises. Each day I would go to the "Upper Room" and wrestle with God. Each day I would come out of those times refreshed, filled with the Spirit of God and resting in Jesus my Sabbath. The words of the Bible would come to life for me. The fear would disappear and the peace of God would flood my soul. Greater clarity would come to me as I studied the Word. Those sections of the Bible that I had always had to explain away were now alive and full of joy and truth for me.

Each day the same pattern occurred. I would wake up in fear, cry out to God, head to the secret place, my "upper room," to meet with Him and pour out my heart to Him. Each day the promises and truths of God's Word, the peace and the joy, would flow over me. I can't say exactly how long this went on, but I know it was many months. Then one day, during my prayer time, God got through to me. It was not an audible voice, just a clear voice in my mind, as if He had spoken out loud to me. "Where is all the fear coming from, Greg? It is coming from the Adventism of your childhood! Where is the joy and peace and freedom coming from? It is coming from My Word and from time spent with Me in this place! Fear is not from Me. My perfect love casts out fear." Suddenly it all became clear. The battle inside me was over. The Spirit of God had set me free. I recognized the bondage I had been in all my life. The veil had fallen from my eyes!

Meanwhile, Paula was coming to the same conclusions on her own. We knew that God was calling us to a deeper walk with Him that would involve stepping out of all that meant security for us. We'd thought at first that God might want us to remain in the church and work for change. However, as we prayed more and more, we became uncomfortable with that option. We are a team that God has uniquely gifted to reach the unchurched. In addition, we have been given leadership and teaching gifts. To know the truth and to just sit on it and hope for change did not seem to fit the way God had wired us. We were willing to do so, however. It sure would be less traumatic.

The other side of the issue for me was the responsibility I have to teach the truth. I am a flawed human being, with so many frailties, but God is doing a great work in my heart. I cannot live a double life. I am not an eloquent speaker or a flashy personality. The only things I have going for me are my convictions and my love for Jesus. If I cannot speak from the core of my experience with Jesus, I am nothing.

Paula and I also felt convinced that it would be wrong to continue to represent an organization that we no longer believed represented truth. To continue to serve in it would be to lend credibility to its claims. We had many wonderful friends in the Seventh-day Adventist Church. We were grateful for our conference president, associate pastors, staff, elders, volunteers, and so many others who had supported us and gone out on a limb to help us try to build a church for a new generation. We did not want to hurt them or the Foster Memorial Church that we loved so much and had given so much of our hearts to over the past eight years. But we knew we had to follow the Lord's leading. We recognized that there would be those who would strongly disagree with our understanding of Scripture and our sense of calling. But we knew that we were not responsible to them. We were responsible to God. We could not remain evangelical Adventists. The box of Adventism excluded too many of God's people.

While the implications of these discoveries were frightening, there was also a sense of eager anticipation as we looked forward to what God had in mind for us. We were being asked to live on the ragged edge of faith. We had to trust in God's promises as never before. We were truly learning to live by faith and *rest* in Jesus, our Lord and Friend. For us, this was no longer just theory, but it was an actual faith experience. It became trust in God's Word and reliance on Him and Him alone. This was to be Sabbath *rest* on a daily basis. We were grateful that God has entrusted us with His truth and allowed us to put Him to the test. Despite our fears, we were confident of the future. Where God leads, He provides. We were about to embark on a **F**antastic **A**dventure **I**n **T**rusting **H**im – **FAITH.**

CHAPTER SIXTEEN

AFTER ADVENTISM

When our family left the Seventh-day Adventist Church, we did not know where we were going or how we would survive. We just knew that God would supply all our needs. What we did not know is how painful, yet rewarding this process would turn out to be. We had many friends in the SDA Church who have a true grasp of the Gospel. These friends understood our process and would often tell us privately that they were in a decision process themselves. When we left the Foster Memorial Church, we did so making every effort to keep the ministry there intact and to leave with grace and kindness. We did share our scriptural journey with the church family in a "Letter to Family and Friends." We resigned as peacefully as we knew how. We did not have any hard feelings against anyone. Our experience with the church had been positive.[1]

Once we left, however, we truly felt the barbs of rejection that are rooted in a theology of exclusivity taught in Seventh-day Adventism. While some of our close friends

[1] See *Resignation Letter* at the end of Chapter Seventeen.

remained close, the majority basically ignored us after that, or avoided us because of our position regarding the Sabbath and the church. It was as if we had a disease. While SDAs do not practice open shunning, they do make their displeasure crystal clear. It was a painful season. Many terrible rumors were circulated about us. We got accusatory and unkind mail telling us we were going to hell and taking our kids with us. One major name in the SDA Church sent a letter out characterizing me as mentally unstable and twisting my statements in an effort to discredit me. There was so much more, but I do not want to dwell on the negative. I must point out, however, that we saw a side of Adventism that made us realize that the SDA Church, as a whole, is still far away from a truly evangelical stance when it comes to Sabbath observance, recognizing the experience and scriptural understanding of other Christians, and moving away from sectarianism. While we knew that leaving the SDA Church would be painful, we had no idea how much so it would be. We realized that those in the SDA Church have their own fears to work through. They don't intentionally want to hurt others, they just fear deception.

On the positive side, however, the Lord gave us so many confirmations of His leading that enabled us to endure the loneliness and rejection that we felt from so many whom we had loved and served over the years. On the day we resigned, one of the associate pastors came to me and told me that he had been praying for us, and in doing so, a picture came to his mind of Jesus with His arms around us. He told me that he was sure that God was leading us and would be taking care of us.

Later on in the week we got a letter from a friend. She wrote that she had been praying for us and had kept hearing in her mind that God loved us and was taking us to a richer place with Him. Then she told me, "Jesus has seen you in the 'Upper Room' and has answered your prayers." Wow! What a confirmation! She had no idea about my "Upper Room."

That was a secret place between God and me. Joy filled my heart!

We started to attend a little church in town. On our first Sunday a woman came up to us all excited. First, she asked me if I remembered her. I told her that I did not. She proceeded to tell me that she had attended my church some time before and that she had met me briefly after the service. Soon after that she had been impressed that she should pray for me. She had sensed God telling her, "Pray for this man. He will obey Me." She proceeded to pray for Paula and me every day. She told me that for two years she had been praying intensely for us and that God would wake her up, sometimes at 2:00 in the morning to pray for us! Wow! All that time I had felt alone in this struggle to follow and listen to God, I was not alone. Our family was not alone. God had sent a prayer warrior to stand with us who we did not even know. What an awesome God!

During the first few days after we resigned, we learned that our severance package, which should have been for six and one third months' salary, was reduced to two and one half months' salary. We had no resources to fall back on. Paula had been working only part-time since we had chosen for her to be a stay-at-home mom. What were we to do? I left with no job prospects. At first we thought we should take legal action to get the rest of the money, but we both felt, after praying about it, that we should rather wait on the Lord for His provision. We did not want to do anything that might jeopardize our witness to Seventh-day Adventists in the future. Very soon after we made that decision we received a call from a friend out west. He had been talking about our resignation with some of his friends. One of them, whom we had never met, was sending us a check for more than a month's salary!

During the seven and one half months without work God did a powerful work in us. We saw the hand of God's provision in such miraculous ways that our faith grew to a whole new level. We also became a part of a church in our area that had a dynamic prayer ministry. This little church adopted us and poured love and acceptance into our lives. We started going to the church during the week for prayer and discovered anew the healing power of prayer. The fear and wounds of the rejection that we had been experiencing melted away when God's people surrounded us in prayer. The joy of the Lord in our hearts started blossoming as never before. Soon we were serving in that prayer ministry and discovering new depths of prayer and walking in the Spirit that we had never tapped into before. Every day our joy in the Lord grew in spite of our circumstances. Our whole worship experience began to deepen. Soon we were asking ourselves why we had missed all of this joy while in the SDA church.

The answer came one day while I was studying Galatians. (I just couldn't get enough of Galatians!) In Chapter 4 the Apostle Paul writes about the blessing of Isaac versus the blessing of Ishmael. As long as Law is in the picture, there is bondage. But when we truly let go of Law and move into grace, we begin to experience the blessing and laughter (Isaac means laughter) of Isaac. The Holy Spirit is so gentle. He does not push Himself on any one. When we hold onto Law, He is still with us. He is just limited in how much He can do in our lives. But when we let go of Law and trust Him fully, He is released in greater power into our lives. Does this make us less sincere in our walk with the Lord? Absolutely not! We find ourselves more careful to follow Him, but our focus is no longer on the Law but on Jesus. The joy of the Lord becomes our strength!

After those seven and one half months, God opened a door for us to serve in a new church plant in Hagerstown, Maryland. The church is sponsored by the Brethren in Christ, an open-minded evangelical denomination with a heart for church planting. The church is now almost three years old. At the time of this writing, I am working with the planting pastor in developing the small group and spiritual gift ministries, as well as mobilizing the new congregation for prayer. It has been an incredible experience as we have watched the church grow. We have just launched a new satellite congregation 15 minutes away on the north side of town. God has abundantly blessed this new congregation with many new faces. Crossroads church now meets at these two locations with a desire to start more churches in the future as God leads. The church has a true heart for evangelism and is composed of new believers, those from various denominations, and many from unchurched backgrounds. The passion for prayer and the heart for worship are contagious. We are now settled into a new home, and God has truly supplied every need and more. We continue to praise God every day for His mighty work in our lives and for the joy and fullness of the Spirit. May His name be praised!

CHAPTER SEVENTEEN

CONCLUSION

What are Seventh-day Adventists? Are they just a group of basically mainline Christians with some unique doctrines? Or should they be classified as a cult group with teachings that should be considered dangerous? My answer to that question is summed up in another question. Would the Apostle Paul have considered the Judaizers, the ones who were leading the Galatians away from the true Gospel, a cult? Most people would answer yes to that question. The Galatians had come under a "bewitching" influence. They had believed "another gospel" that was really not a gospel at all. These teachers were causing the Galatians to "fall from grace." They were courting them for "no good." These false teachers were putting the people back under a "yoke of bondage."

The Galatians' heresy was subtle. At first it seemed genuine because it taught that people were saved by grace. In Galatians 3 we read:

> O foolish Galatians! Who has bewitched you that you should not obey the truth, before whose eyes Jesus Christ was clearly portrayed among you as crucified? This only I want to learn from you: *Did you receive the*

Spirit by the works of the law, or by the hearing of faith? Are you so foolish? Having begun in the Spirit, are you now being made perfect by the flesh? Gal. 3:1-3

The Galatians heresy did not teach that people come to Christ by the works of the Law. It taught that one must come to Christ by faith alone. So far so good! *But*—here is the subtle twist—after coming to Christ and receiving the Spirit by faith, they were then taught that they were required to keep the Law, specifically circumcision, the food laws, and the Sabbath laws. These were to be kept in order to *maintain* salvation. That is what made the Galatians' heresy so subtle and bewitching. It taught grace to start out with, but soon it took away the joy and freedom by *requiring specific laws in order to remain saved.*

This was the Galatian heresy, and I am convinced that the Seventh-day Adventist Church embodies the modern day version of it. While SDAs do not require law in order to be saved, they do require it in order to remain saved. They may not require circumcision like the Judaizers did, but they do require the food laws and the Sabbath. In fact, this requirement, specifically the Sabbath observance on Saturday is to them the sign that distinguishes them as God's last true remnant church. All other churches and Christians are outside of God's will and must one day submit to the Sabbath teaching or be lost. While those who do not understand this might be saved outside of Adventism, no one who has been exposed to this "truth" and does not stay with it, will be saved.

There are some Adventists who are not pushy about their beliefs. There are some who are not out to convert others into their particular brand of Christianity. There were several like this in the church we had pastored. Once we had been asked to resign, I sat down with the elders and discussed our journey and the scriptural reasons for our convictions. Several of them had read the appendix to our resignation letter that included much of the Bible study covered in this book. One of the elders, in particular, was concerned that it not get into the hands of the members because it might shake their faith in the Adventist system. He pointed out that there are various theological viewpoints that people can choose from regarding the Old and New Covenant. Many believe the Old Covenant (specifically the Sabbath) is just rewritten in the heart of believers in the New Covenant. Many believe that the Ten Commandments have been here for eternity past and will be in force for eternity future. "You just have a different view. So what difference does it make? Isn't what you are sharing just another viewpoint?"

I responded with two key points. I told him, "The idea that the Old Covenant (specifically the Ten Commandments including the fourth) is eternal and is just written in the heart in the New Covenant is a nice concept except for the fact that nowhere does the Bible teach this to be true. In fact, Galatians specifically tells us it is *not* true. Secondly, and more importantly, this very issue came up in Acts 15. Some of the Jewish believers insisted that the Gentile believers be required to be circumcised and keep the Law of Moses. The early church leaders refused to compromise the Gospel and place a yoke of bondage on the new believers that they themselves had been unable to bear. What would have happened to the spread of Christianity had they given in to these Jewish believers and required the new believers to become Jewish in order to be Christian? It would have destroyed the evangelistic power of the early church. Christianity would have been severely crippled. It would have become just another Jewish sect rather than the massive world religion it is today. If they had not stood strong on the truth of the Gospel, it is probable that none of us would be believers today. We are Gentiles. If it was that important then, it is just as important today. I told them, "It would personally be much easier for my family and me just to compromise, keep our mouths shut, teach the things we hold in common with other Christians, and just go along with the denomination—but at what cost? If the Gospel was important enough for the early church council to face the criticism of the Jewish believers, then it must be important for us today."

What about the billboards I mentioned in the introduction equating Sunday worship with the Mark of the Beast? Are these a true reflection of what the Adventist Church teaches or are they just the extreme views of a few radicals in the far right wing of the church? Actually before we left Adventism we heard denominational leaders express their concerns over these signs and the occasional full page advertisements in newspapers. They are not happy with those who have taken it upon themselves to put these out in the public eye. The concerns, however, are not because they do not believe these things to be true. They have issue with the timing. They would prefer to have this come out after seven or eight nights in a *Revelation Seminar* or a *Prophecy Crusade* when people have had a chance to hear some more general Bible teaching and have let their defenses down. The billboards do represent Adventist teaching. It is the timing that concerns the church leaders.

Are there evangelical Adventists who do not believe they are the one true church? Are there people in Adventism who observe Sabbath only as a spiritual discipline and not as a moral command? Yes, there are. But this is not the official stance of the church. In the October, 2002 North American Division edition of the *Adventist Review*, General Conference President Jan Paulsen wrote these words.

> We shun the perception of being arrogant, and we don't want to come across as being overly exclusive, but at the same time we believe that being *Seventh-day Adventists* has direct bearing on our salvation; that while a believer can be saved as a Catholic, I would risk my whole

> spiritual life and salvation were I to leave what I am now and join any other community.[1]

Further, toward the conclusion of the article, Jan Paulsen, President of the General Conference of Seventh-day Adventists, says regarding historic Adventism,

> Some would have us believe that there have been significant shifts in recent times in regard to doctrines that historically have been at the heart of Adventism. Take specifically our understanding of the judgment and Christ's ministry in the heavenly sanctuary, and the prophetic messages in which these teachings are contained.... nothing could be further from the truth. The historic sanctuary message, based on the scripture and supported by the writings of Ellen White, continues to be held unequivocally.[2]

What does he mean by the *sanctuary message*? He means the idea of an investigative judgment of believers before Christ comes that determines salvation. This sanctuary doctrine in Adventism first led them to predict that Jesus would come in 1844, and then when He did not come, to say that the Old Covenant style Day of Atonement began in heaven on that date. It was out of this teaching that the Sabbath emphasis came. By causing Adventists to focus on the Old Covenant *sanctuary*, they became fascinated with the Ten Commandments, and eventually the seventh-day Sabbath. This is the very core of the problem in Adventism. The Adventist emphasis on the Old Covenant has caused them to insist on Sabbath observance and food laws that the New Covenant clearly warns Christians not to do. Has Adventism changed? Is it becoming part of the Christian

[1] Jan Paulsen, *Adventist Review*, October 2002, p 34.
[2] Ibid, p. 37

community? According to the President of the world church, it is not.

Seventh-day Adventism has made many good and healthy contributions to the world. One of the most extensive hospital systems has been developed by the SDA Church. There are healthy lifestyle issues that Adventists have championed. They have developed a worldwide educational system. From the outside looking in, there is much that is appealing. However, Paul warns that even if an angel from heaven teaches another gospel let him be accursed.

Paula and I have a deep heart and love for the Adventist Church. We long for the hearts and minds of all who are in that system to come to grips with the truth of the Gospel. There is not a day that goes by that we do not pray for the people to whom we will always be bonded by a common past, family and friendships. We can understand Paul's heart for his people. We pray and will keep on praying until the walls are broken down and all God's people are truly set free!

I will close by including the final segment of our letter to family and friends, and that we distributed to our church elders upon our resignation from the Adventist pastorate. These sentiments still reflect our heart for the Seventh-day Adventist Church and our prayer for honesty and revival in that community.

Resignation Letter July 28, 2001

Paula and I have a deep love and concern for the Adventist church. We have not been hurt or mistreated. We do not hold animosity toward anyone in the church. The denomination has been very good to us. We do not have any horror stories of mistreatment by leadership as some have. We are grateful for Adventism and what it has meant to our family and our growth in the Lord. Virtually all of our maturing process as Christians has taken place within the Adventist church. We have been blessed deeply by our association with the church. But God is calling us to keep moving. I believe that is His intention for the Adventist church as well. There truly was merit in what the Adventist pioneers believed. They were adamant about not becoming another denomination but insisted in calling themselves a movement. By this they were indicating that if they discovered more truth, they would follow it and leave the mistakes behind. The Adventist church has much to offer. If it would keep moving, I believe it could have a tremendous impact on the world as a part of God's remnant church at large. But in a very real sense, Adventism must face its dark side. It must keep moving and allow God to mold and make it into what He intends it to be.

We are probably more "adventist" than we have ever been. I mean, of course, that we are passionate about the soon return of Jesus. This is why it is time, high time, that all churches stop promoting their own brand of Christianity as the "only true" exclusive community, and instead band together for the common cause of reaching the world for Jesus. This was the passion of Jesus in John 15. "By this will all men know that you are my disciples if you love one another." The mark of true Christian maturity is this love for one another and getting on with taking the message of Jesus to the world. Jesus' prayer in John 17 makes clear that He longs for the unity of His church. It is this unity that will attract the world to Jesus Christ. When Christians fight among themselves it only reaffirms unbelievers in their impression that Christianity is just another human institution.

Unity in purpose is what the true remnant of Bible prophecy is all about. In all my years of ministry I can never recall any of us rejoicing over the success of a Billy Graham Crusade. I never heard anyone praising God that Greg Laurie had a successful Harvest Crusade. I must include myself in this group. Why?—because these men weren't part of the "true church." This attitude can unfortunately be found in many church systems. This is not just an SDA phenomenon. I have had to take a hard look at my own attitudes over the years. We believe that the time has come for us to lay aside the exclusivism that has crippled the Christian church for centuries (see Gal. 4:17) and get on with the Gospel Commission (Mt. 28:18-20). We are convinced that this is Jesus' dream for His church in these last days. We believe that the highest form of worship, the most God-honoring path we can choose is to follow Jesus as He leads us. We believe that His remnant are those who obey His commandments to love Him fully, love others as themselves, and are totally sold out to telling the world about Him.

As I write this, I do not know what the future will hold. I do not know what will happen to us financially. I must say that there was a real sense in which I had to face a dark part of my own personality in this struggle. I valued being a respected SDA pastor and having people think well of me. To think that others whom I had known and served in Adventism might lose respect for me was incredibly difficult for me to accept. I had to, in a very real sense, repent for having loved the praise of men more than the praise of God. Now I am resolved that "as for me and my house, we will serve the Lord." We will find our rest and security in Him. And we will look forward to seeing how God leads us and how he leads all of you in the months and years that follow. Our prayers are with you, and we solicit your prayers for us.

We hope that someday the Adventist church will face some of these issues. We pray that one day soon there will be a courageous move made on the part of the leadership to reexamine the "pillars of the faith" and ask God to give them the courage to study openly, without risk, the fundamental teachings and see what the scriptures teach without worrying what will happen if there is a discovery that there have been some mistakes along the way. It takes courage to face difficult issues. But courage is one of the qualities that

Adventists have been noted for in the past. We are confident that the same quality still exists.

We do not think the church will suffer long term from such a study. Perhaps the image that the Adventists are the one and only remnant church would fall by the wayside. Perhaps the Investigative Judgment would hit the theological grave yard too. There might be a whole new approach to the Sabbath. It might be that Sabbath would be a suggested spiritual discipline rather than a moral ought. The name "Seventh-day Adventist" might be reduced to just "Adventist" so as to keep the focus on Jesus rather than the law. Healthful living might be taught from a suggested lifestyle approach rather than a requirement that gets confused with salvation. Maybe the church could become known as a church that truly is based on the Bible and the Bible alone. Perhaps there might even be some apologies made to those Christian groups that have been cut down and abused by the "evangelists" who called them "Apostates" and "Babylon"! Maybe the focus in evangelism would shift toward reaching the 130 million unchurched people in this country instead of primarily those already connected to a church family. Perhaps the Adventists around the globe would become known as a people passionate about reaching people for Jesus, cooperative in connecting with other Christian groups, and totally unselfish in using the church's massive resources for the cause of Christ.

Maybe all of this sounds like a dream, but can you imagine how God could bless an organization with that kind of courage and authenticity? Imagine how spiritual seekers and believers alike would respect such authentic spirituality. But it will not happen if there are not at least a few that are praying for true revival and unity in the body of Christ, the unity that comes when all true Christians take John 17 seriously. When Christians start loving one another and telling the good news to the world instead of clumping in little exclusive denominational groups and pretending they are the only ones, there will be a revival of mammoth proportions. It will not happen, however, if there are not at least a few that are willing to stand up and speak their minds. We happen to know that there are many SDAs among the grass roots, including some pastors, administrators, and teachers, that have this heart. But nothing will happen as long as it just takes place in little discussions in the back rooms. Some of us need to have the courage to speak up and tell the truth. Someday we believe that God is going to accomplish these things in Adventism. We will be praying daily for just such a revival.

Love to all of you,
In Christ Jesus our Security and Rest,

Greg and Paula Taylor

Helpful Web Sites

www.ellenwhite.org

http://members.tripod.com/~Help_for_SDAs/index.html

www.ratzlaf.com

www.sdaoutreach.org

www.formeradventist.com

www.oneflockministries.org

One Flock Ministries is an inter-denominational ministry encouraging the cooperation of Bible believing Christians in reaching the world for Jesus Christ. We long for Christ's heart for unity in His church to be realized in our generation. We are part of the worldwide prayer movement seeking revival and renewal around the world. We have a special passion for helping those caught in sectarian systems to find freedom in Christ and community with other believers for the sake of the advancement of the kingdom. We desire to provide Bibles, books, training and study materials to enable people in impoverished areas of the world to plant non-sectarian churches and small group networks. Should you have an interest in helping us accomplish these goals you may visit our website at www.oneflockministries.org. You can make tax deductible contributions to EndowmentBuilders Foundation, Inc. FBO One Flock Ministries. Send all correspondence to One Flock Ministries, 10730 Bratton Court, Williamsport, MD 21795

OTHER BOOKS PUBLISHED BY LIFE ASSURANCE MINISTRIES PUBLICATIONS

SABBATH IN CHRIST

Dale Ratzlaff, 438 pages, $14.95

John MacArthur Ph.D., Senior Pastor, Grace Community Church, Sun Valley, California, "I'm impressed with the clarity, precision, and thoroughness of Dale Ratzlaff's work. This book is a much-needed treatment of the Sabbath controversy, written with intelligent passion and full of insight and wisdom. Mr. Ratzlaff shows great care in his handling of the complex biblical, historical, and theological issues. This book will be a great encouragement and help to anyone struggling to understand what Scripture says about the Sabbath."

Joseph Tkach, D.Min., Pastor General, Worldwide church of God, "We believe the foundational texts, concepts and ideas you discuss are thoroughly supported by the biblical witness. They are also clearly presented. Your explanation that Christ is the basis of New Testament law ('the law of Christ') is excellent. Perhaps nothing is as vital to understanding the Sabbath question as the fact that the old covenant and Mosaic law must be interpreted by the new covenant and read in a Christ-centered way. Your consistent explication of this principle is absolutely necessary and correct....I pray that *Sabbath in Christ* will be instrumental in opening hearts and minds to the truth of the gospel message that our Sabbath is the eternal spiritual rest we have in our Lord."

THE CULTIC DOCTRINE OF SEVENTH-DAY ADVENTISTS

Dale Ratzlaff, 388 pages, $14.95

Timothy Oliver, Editor, Researcher at Watchman Fellowship, "Ratzlaff's writing clearly possesses a spirit of meekness; it is nevertheless a tour de force. Patiently pursuing his subject, he lays out the evidence supporting an irresistible conclusion—Ellen White was not a true prophet or messenger from God, and the Seventh-day Adventist Church is not what it claims to be, the only true "remnant church." If Adventist leadership will heed his plea, then perhaps this church is salvageable. If not, then it is time for evangelicals everywhere to say to the Christians within Adventism, with neither malice nor exultation, but with one united and very earnest voice, "Babylon is fallen! Come out of her my people!"

A Theologian's Journey from Seventh-day Adventism to Mainstream Christianity

Jerry Gladson, Ph.D., 383 pages, $14.95

Dr. Gladson was a SDA theologian, professor and pastor serving an important role at the central core of Adventist scholarship for many years. Drawing from his meticulously kept journals, Dr. Gladson describes events at the center of the recent crisis in Adventism. He has done something few other scholars have been able to do. He has combined careful, detailed research with a gripping, narrative style of writing. The reader is forced to crawl under the skin of Dr. Gladson, see through his eyes and feel the trauma of having to choose between career and conscience. One cannot put the book down until finished. This book uncovers the hidden, toxic core of Adventism.

White Washed, Uncovering the Myths of Ellen G. White

Sydney Cleveland, 233 pages, $12.95

White Washed is a comprehensive look at Ellen White's prophecies, practices and publications. Sydney Cleveland examines her claims of inspiration, her dreams and visions, the doctrines she endorsed, her personal practices that opposed her teachings and the effect of her claims on the Adventist Church. This is a well-documented overview of the little-known reality about Ellen White and her long service to the Adventist church. Sydney Cleveland was an Adventist pastor for 11 years. During an extensive study of Ellen G. White's writings, he discovered that she contradicted the Holy Bible, gave many false prophecies, and didn't even follow her own teachings.

The Sabbath and the Lord's day

H. M. Riggle, 160 pages $7.95

This book includes a discussion of Sabbath/Sunday issues in the early church and is an excellent companion to *Sabbath in Christ.*

Life Assurance Ministries Publications also sells a number of other books, videos and tapes not listed here. For a current list please go to our LAM Bookstore at www.ratzlaf.com/lam_book.htm.